Ode to Bermuda Grass

Ashley,

There are not enough words to describe how much you friendship means to me.

Love you!

Julie

Ode to Bermuda Grass: My Journey Through Loss, Grief and Adoption

By
Julie Yackley

First Edition: August 2018
Cover Art by A. Seiler
Edited by Kathy Hadel
Printed in the United States of America
ISBN-139781642544633

To my children, always and forever, no matter what. To my KAD family and friends, thank you for being such an amazing support.

Preface

When I was in middle school I began to keep a diary this would eventually lead me to journal about anything and everything. When I got the idea to write this book I didn't expect to finish it. Honestly, when I had discussed this idea with my friends I had assumed it would be one of the many projects I would start and never finish. Looks like I was wrong, completely. This book has been very therapeutic for me; I've been able to put down my experiences in a way that I hope will help others. Once I had been able to pinpoint where the self-sabotaging behavior came from and how to control it and heal from it I wanted everyone to know about it. For years I believed that I would forever be stuck in my pattern, leaving a trail of broken hearts and failed relationships behind me. There was so much relief knowing that I would be able to heal from the inside out, that there was hope for those who confided in me that also self-sabotaged. This book is for those people, the ones who have not yet realized that there is hope and healing, that your past will not define you. Inside each of us lies the ability to overcome anything that life has thrown at you. I am living proof no matter the circumstances, you are not your circumstances, and those do not define you. Inside of each of us in an insurmountable power, and we just have to be courageous enough to use it.

Chapter 1

"You can't go back and change the beginning, but you can start where you are and change the ending." - C.S. Lewis

Everyone's childhood is a little different and although there are some parallels, not all have been infiltrated by grief, loss, emotionally unavailable people, constant criticism and rejection. Those who have experienced loss, trauma, constant criticism or abandonment do not speak up. Their pain stays hidden inside away from the world isolating themselves from the world around them. The voices of these people go unheard out of fear they will be judged, criticized and further isolated from those around them. They believe they are alone as if no one else in the world will understand what they have gone through or the feelings they continue to conceal.

We bury our pain in the very depths of our being; we hide the scars on our hearts and minimize the impact our childhood or our past has had on who we are today. While masquerading around with smiles on our faces believing that we are just like everyone else. Pretending we are like everyone else hurts us from the inside out as we continue to deny who we really are. We ignore the feelings inside, pushing them down praying they will leave us alone. Beneath the surface lies a web of weeds and roots, twisting around our feelings, our hearts and hijacking our thoughts.

Our relationships succumb to the ensnarement of these roots, limiting us with others while suffocating us hindering any progress we try to make. My childhood is not one of constant grey clouds; there were very bright areas of sunshine and happiness. The impact that has affected me is the instances of grey clouds, the times were the sun did not shine as bright.

Reflecting back on my childhood years, it is unlike others, while there are moments of great achievement, happiness and success, there are also low moments of loss, rejection, consistent criticism and judgment. At the age of six months, I was adopted from South Korea. The information I have on my biological parents is rather limited. What I do know is that my biological father's name and details are unknown, at least on paper. My biological mother has more details however if those details are factual, I may never know. My adoptive parents, I do know, my mom was a teacher for children with special needs, and my dad owned his own business doing home improvements, specifically siding windows and doors.

Their details I know, that they met while doing a local company play, my mom was working on her Master's degree and my dad had previously gone to trade school in Austin, MN. On May 15, 1986, I arrived in Minnesota accompanied by my social worker to meet my adoptive parents. There are days that I look at pictures from that day, the happiness on their faces was undeniable, in those first few moments, and nothing else mattered in the word. My presence had completed their family, I had arrived home.

Within a short few years, my little world would be turned upside down and my life would forever change. My mom lost her battle when I was seven after a grueling fight, radiation, chemotherapy, double mastectomy and the vast variety of diets and self-healing tapes. She fought a courageous battle even at the end, convinced she would recover and overcome cancer. Losing a parent so young forever changes who you become, it shapes you in a way that only others who have lost a parent will understand. Your parent is forever remembered in your mind as you saw them, I held my mom on a pedestal. She was my hero and I will always remember her as a fighter, a warrior and brave.

The feeling of loss is not something anyone is able to describe or empathize with, unless you know what it feels like, words of empathy can fall on deaf ears. There are no words that are able to comfort those that have lost a parent unless you yourself have gone through the same loss.

The first funeral I can remember was when I was four. My mother's father died suddenly at home. Being so young, there is not very much that I remember, except I remember hearing that my grandparents were home, my grandma was in the kitchen. My grandpa told her he was going to lie down or didn't feel good, something to that effect. She found him lying on the bed. Death was still a foreign concept for me to understand. Growing up going to Sunday school, I understood what death meant but fully grasping the concept was still new. There are few memories with my grandpa. Mostly they include him, my grandma and my uncles at the time smoking outside of our house. My mom refused to let them smoke inside. During part of the funeral, I played a song I had learned while taking piano lessons and wanted to play it for him. I can remember my mom beaming with pride as I played; she had the biggest smile on her face. This was my first experience of loss, the first time I remember encountering death and grief while not really experiencing it myself.

Following his funeral just three short years later, I would be at my mom's funeral. I wouldn't be the same. By this time cancer and treatments had distorted her face and body. Her face was bigger and she had lost all of her hair. No longer remained the dark hair I saw in pictures or her slim face. During the funeral, I remember my dad holding me and several people giving us their sympathy and expressing condolences. As my family began preparing a bulletin board of pictures, I look a piece of paper and started to draw. Once the picture was completed, I gave it to my dad and explained what I had drawn. My picture was of my mom, she was in between two angels who were bringing her up into the heavens, and she was crying. Beneath the three of them was me, screaming "Don't go". My dad made that the center of the bulletin board.

Years later he would have the picture framed and in his office. Remembering the painful parts of my childhood and adolescence brings up old scars and stirs old familiar feelings. However, I believe that my story and what I have been through while knowing that we all have the strength to overcome the old hurts and pain from our past. Being aware of our issues is one thing, being able to confront our issues head on like a gardener does while weeding flower beds is another. Like the gardener, you will get dirty, it is hard work, work that will almost break you, the tears will flow and everything you thought you know will be shaken, down to your foundation. Like the gardener every weed needs to be pluck from the flowerbed, each root of that weed needs to be dug out as well. It is laborious work and takes time there is no rush and no race to complete but without weeding out your garden, the weeds overtake your flowers just as pain from your past can overtake and destroy your life.

Abandonment -- a word that no one likes to talk about, a word that people associate with growing up in a single parent home because one of them left. It is a word that usually goes hand in hand with the term “daddy issues”; that I never associated with rejection, disappointment or even unmet needs until I worked through an abandonment workbook. Most people don’t want to associate themselves with this word due to the negative connotation, even myself. It was something I could ignore and rationalize how something like that never affected me.

This word continues to be used to describe girls with low self-esteem, who engage in risky and casual behaviors with others because their dad's left and they didn't have a positive male role model in her life. Our society continues to validate that this is the only explanation for abandonment by using this type of context in TV shows or movies. There is no surprise that no one wants to openly admit something like this, to be labeled as damaged goods, until now. Over the last couple of years, I have struggled to try to pinpoint the source of my feelings and explanation of the self-sabotaging behaviors I have engaged in over the years. Eventually, I had to come to terms with identifying with abandonment, there are days that I still struggle the push the word out of my mouth.

Even while going on this journey of healing and self-discovery there are instances where I still try not to find associations with this word, where I try and find alternatives to explain why I made the decision I have in my past. Abandonment is not just a parent leaving the home and cutting off all contact, usually in early childhood. The idea of abandonment is complex with many different layers and definitions. Because people experience trauma and loss in different ways with different events being traumatic it is not a surprise that abandonment is the same way.

Abandonment can happen as a child or as an adult; because we have formed attachments with people throughout our lives it is not shocking to think that if those people were to ever leave our lives we would on some level feel abandoned, even if it was an unhealthy relationship. Never would I have thought that I would eventually identify with this word but after following all the roots beneath the surface, I found that most of my struggles all stemmed from this place. Growing up all I knew is that I was adopted by two parents who loved me. Abandonment was never a word that I associated with needs that were left unmet or constant rejection. The concept of associating these things with abandonment continue to be new to me, but important nonetheless. Without the complex definition and explanation of how this affects your behaviors, my life would be worse off without the ability to label the very root of my sabotaging behavior. Without the association with this word, I would have most likely spent my entire life ensuring that I was unhappy and alone while to isolate myself from the world around me.

The summer of 2017 would be a poignant time of self-discovery and healing. The weekend started off pretty mundane, waking up to my kids crawling into bed and moving around so much that being able to get back to sleep was unrealistic. Like most weekend mornings it started with making a cup of coffee and making sure my children and their dad had breakfast. The plan for the day was to just do yard work and get the flowers beds weeded; we were still trying to figure out where to put the garden. That Saturday was hot, humid and sunny; there wasn't a cloud in the sky. Without thinking I didn't put sunscreen on and ended up with a bright pink sunburned back with the outline of my tank top. Starting out wasn't too bad, most were your typical weeds, easy to pull out as long as you used most of your strength.

Then I stumbled upon what appeared to be grass. At first, you would pull it up and there would be long sections of mini grass shoots and a few roots. I remember thinking to myself how easy this was going to be, man was I wrong. Eventually, after pulling up this weed several times, it began going deeper and deeper into the ground. It was able to penetrate through tree roots and get tangled up in its own root system. Most of the time I needed to dig the damn roots out because just pulling on it wasn't enough. If you were lucky enough to get some roots, there would be others in several different directions weaving in-between other roots, other plants, rocks, and even concrete.

Have you ever tried to dig up or pull out Bermuda grass? It is an absolute pain in the ass. Each time I would pull up some roots there would be another segment and deeper roots. It was never ending. As soon as I started to weed through the flower bed, I became obsessed to figure out where the beginning of this weed began. It looked never ending. I wanted to find it and dig the entire thing up. After many Google searches, I found out that it was a type of Bermuda grass, the type of root system it has and how to successfully get rid of it. After reading different websites regarding this "grass," there were two options: I could either dig it up, or put a plastic sheet over the area and let the sun kill everything beneath it. Since this specific type of grass could go as deep as six feet into the ground and even survive a drought it was recommended to use the plastic to kill it. This damn thing could survive a drought?! I had my work cut out for me. Clearly covering a flower bed with a plastic sheet wouldn't be very productive since there were bushes and flowers that were also there. My only choice was to dig it up and pull it out.

As I pulled it up I noticed that it would grow along the ground and wind itself around other root systems, usually trees, crabgrass, and bushes. The roots would get tangled around themselves while weaving back and forth creating new plants along the way. Then the roots would move deeper into the ground, ensuring that it was deep enough to survive a drought. It was a nasty weed; the roots and stems went deep and were hard to pull out like they had the ability to hold themselves in the dirt. My entire afternoon was spent digging up the ground and revealing long segments of weeds and roots and pulling my hardest to remove them if digging around them didn't work. The day ended with my back being sunburned and my hands covered in blisters and only a small area of the flower bed weeded. If you looked it wouldn't seem like much progress, in fact, I was pretty disappointed that I wasn't able to pull out more roots. At the time it never crossed my mind that I would reflect back on this afternoon as a parallel to my life.

By now I'm sure you're wondering how the hell I can find meaning in weeding a flower bed to my life. This weed became my arch nemesis and my mission was to eradicate it from my flower beds. This story is no fairy tale. This is my life, my childhood, one that I decided to conquer after a childhood of loss, rejection, isolation and constant criticism which followed me into adolescence and young adulthood. The ability to heal old wounds, rediscover me and shed light in the dark corners of myself has been an uphill battle. In these moments of healing I have stumbled, denied and even made excuses for myself. It is a continual journey of healing.

Chapter 2

"I see what grief does, how it strips you bare, shows you all the things you don't want to know. That loss doesn't end, that there isn't a moment where you are done, when you can neatly put it away and move on"
~ Elizabeth Scott

The only real memories I have of my mom are her in the hospital surrounded my tubes and doctors. Tubing that would stretch across her nose, with an IV placed in her hand and her body covered in a hospital gown. This would be to come how I would always remember her, laying in a hospital bed. The most vivid memories of her are when she was sick after cancer had spread with trips in and out of different hospitals, notes left from her saying the doctors are needing to run more tests to help her get better. During these times if I was not with my dad, then either family or family friends would be taking care of me. My mom had a very close friend, Sally, a mother of one of her students. She had become very close with her and her family, and I remember spending a lot of time with them and their granddaughter Whitney while my mom was sick. There were times Sally even brought me to preschool because my mom would be in the hospital and my dad would be caring for her.

Prior to those vivid memories are pictures of us together where we are fishing off of a dock, her smiling and holding me smiling at Disney World, making sand castles on the beach or just spending time together in our yard. We would take yearly trips in the summer to northern Minnesota, sometimes with her brothers and my grandma. Those photographs are how I want to remember her, but as hard as I try I can't remember those times. All that remains are the stories from others that I have heard that include me in them. Sometimes I wonder if my mind has made some of these memories up, or made up things I remember her telling me. There are days where I am sure without a doubt that she told me that I was going to be like Pippi Longstocking and other days where I ask myself if she even said that. When I was writing in college I mentioned how I felt the rain that day on my face as I watched her coffin get lowered into the ground. Was that real or did I imagine that because it fit my mood that day? After doing some research, my memory is not right. It was not raining and cool that day, it was actually warm and the sun was shining.

This is how I remember my mom, lying in a hospital bed with mouth swab sponges, oxygen tubing across her nose and IVs as she told me I was going to be like Pippi Longstocking, and how much she loved me. At the time I had become obsessed with the movie Pippi Longstocking, the story of a girl who was the daughter of a sea captain and whose mother spoke to her through the clouds. One year for Halloween, my dad even put the wire in my hair so that my pigtails would resemble Pippi's more. I remember how we went to the doctor in Edina to get the screws in her halo tightened and how her face tensed up in pain as the nurses took alcohol swabs to the screws in her forehead prior to tightening them. When my mom was healthy enough to be at home, her dresser would have different wigs on it, both were short brown hair to help hide her bald head.

In my parent's room, my mom had an extra egg crate foam mattress, it was there in case she needed the extra support when she slept. In the afternoon or the evening when I wanted to be closer to her but would be unable to lay next to her, I created my own little bed in the egg crate mattress. I would roll it up and put it on one end and inside that column; I would create a little bed for myself. Since my mom spent a lot of time mainly in two different hospitals, I had become accustomed to the smell. It is a smell I will never be able to associate with anyone else except for my dad. Even now walking into hospitals and being able to smell that sterile smell causes the stomach to plunge to the floor and my anxiety to increase. If I have to go into a hospital now, I have to constantly remind myself that I am okay and it is just a smell, nothing more.

It wasn't until my 20s that I learned my mom had chemotherapy or radiation the morning of my arrival to the states. Every year, while I was in college and after my dad, would call me on my Adoption Birthday, the day I arrived to the states. It wasn't until later into my adult life that my dad would add in little details when he was telling me the story. One year he called me at the exact time he was putting gas into their van, to drive my mom down for her cancer treatment. Another year he called to tell me that he had gone the opposite was on the highway and my mom was yelling at him to turn around because she didn't want to be late. When her and my dad went to the doctor about having kids, the risk because of cancer and the treatments were too great for them to have biological children. From there they decided to adopt, and then I arrived. She continued to fight cancer believing she would be able to conquer it. Even up until the very end she would tell people that she is going to get through this, that she would beat this disease for me.

Around the time I was in kindergarten, my mom wanted to sign me up for a pageant. We sat in the kitchen filling out the application, during this time she probably had her hair and it was probably the healthiest I remember. She asked me who my favorite band was, I didn't know any bands other than the Beach Boys so obviously, that was my answer. After we filled out the application, I anxiously awaited for something to come back in the mail. I daydreamed about walking around in pretty dresses with the hope and possibility of winning and wearing a crown. Unfortunately, that day never came, the day of the competition my mom needed to go to the hospital for more tests or cancer treatment, I can't be sure of which. Obviously, I was disappointed I didn't get to go and walk around in pretty dresses and win a crown, but I knew my mom was sick and I wanted her to get better. From what I can recall my mom was brave, she had a courageous heart. She wore a halo, turtle shell neck brace and other neck braces while she fought her disease. Her faith never wavered.

There is a hospital in Rochester, MN, it is St. Mary's Hospital but I knew it as Mayo. Here is where I would remember spending a lot of days with my mom and dad. When I was little there would be mornings that we would get up early because mom had a doctor appointment. We would walk through the halls that had these three dimensional colored cubes on the sides of the wall and a two way mirror I used to make funny faces in. If my memory serves me correct, I even celebrated a birthday or holiday there, I can still see the brown boxes in her room. Eventually, this hospital would be a place I would forever associate with my mom and cancer, returning there never crossed my mind. In my mind that hospital was a place that I preferred not to think about, the thought of going back to St. Mary's was out of the question. It would have taken an act of God to get me to step foot back into that hospital, and that is exactly what got me to return.

After my dad's diagnosis of ALS, I would eventually have to face the hospital again, something I never thought I would have to do. As I walked through the doors, the smell brought me back to childhood along with the anxiety, I was thankful my friend had driven me down there and I was not there alone. My dad was in a different part of the hospital, it had been so long and I was so young when I was there last that nothing seemed familiar except the smell. In a few moments, my dad and I had alone I asked him if he ever thought we would be back here. He said no, he never thought we would be back at Mayo, much less because he needed the care. For a split second, I thought it would end there, my dad had a rough weekend and I feared he would not be able to get back home. It was not the first time he had stayed in this hospital, but it was the first time I had come to see him and spend the weekend. Thankfully he was able to be discharged and taken back home.

There was a hotel across the street that my dad and I used to stay at when my mom was there. It was called The Bell Tower Inn. It's no longer there but driving down the same street brought back a flood of memories and emotions. It has changed since I've been there. The small little hotel where I would watch The Munsters was gone and in its place was a larger chain hotel. A part of me wanted to walk in, to see if muscle memory would take me to any place familiar.

The fall of 2017, I had to face my worst fear; my dad lost his battle to ALS. The wave of emotions was overwhelming and yet at the time, I felt numb as if nothing had happened and I was in the middle of a nightmare. I wasn't sure how I was going to respond since I had only imagined such a thing happening. In my younger years, I would joke about having to be committed because at the time I could not picture this world without my dad in it. Now I feared that would be my reality, which I would somehow suffer a mental break and would be committed for my own safety. Mentally I was trying to prepare myself to crack, for the bottom to fall out beneath me. Losing one parent, especially so young was difficult enough, now I had to go with losing another. The man who will forever be etched in my mind as any little girl sees her dad, superman.

Looking back and reflecting on everything that surrounded me, I know God walked alongside me. During the time my dad fought the disease, I continued to grow closer to God and continued to stay active in my church family. My dad left this earth with a boom of thunder on a clear night without any clouds surrounded by family. The next morning was a perfect crisp fall morning. The wind was cool enough on your face to remind you that fall was approaching and the sun shined bright in the sky with the leaves turning brilliant colors. Everything in the moment I stood outside taking a sip of coffee was perfect. For a split second, I wanted to run to my dad and tell him it was the perfect fall day. Then reality hit me hard in the chest as if the wind had knocked the air right out of me. He wasn't there; he had already left this earth. I knew the morning was a sign from him; it was the type of morning he loved. He would have been walking around the yard with the dog, getting the newspaper with a cup of coffee in hand. That morning I felt that everything was going to be okay, that I was going to be okay.

I grieved his loss differently than I thought I would and differently than when I lost my mom.

I wasn't that little girl anymore, confused and not fully comprehending what was going on around me. This time I had to explain death to my children, my son was with me when it happened, I watched his eyes well up with tears as I told him his Papa died. My ears will never forget him screaming out “My Papa! I want my Papa!” after I told him. My heart had been broken again, I was okay with going through another loss, for me, it almost seemed like second nature, but watching my son’s little heart break and sobbing in pain broke my heart even more. My world did shatter; more than I ever thought was possible. Patiently and anxiously I wanted for an overwhelming dark spiraling abyss to engulf me and take over my life. The darkness came, but it did not destroy me or take over my life. Somehow I was able to grief the loss every day and still managed to be strong for my children and be the mom they needed.

This time around it had been a lot different. My support system was different, my healing was different. I was different. I had been grieving losing him since the day I heard about his diagnosis. The friends surrounding me allowed me to just grieve when I needed to and would just sit there and listen if I needed it. I am positive that I made it through this season with the help of God and my friends. Most of the time, I said I was running on prayers while clinging to some of my favorite verses in the Bible. This time I was open about what I was dealing with, the struggle to be over a thousand miles away watching your dad suffer from a terminal illness. I leaned on friends that would encourage me with Truth and just tell me how unfair it was. I wasn't ready for him to leave this earth, but I had been able to prepare myself for the inevitable.

The day after my dad passed, we went to the funeral home in town to start planning everything. My hometown has grown since I grew up there, but it still has the small town feel and a lot of people knew my dad. The owner of the funeral home, Steve, also did my mom's funeral and served on the cemetery board at church with my dad. The number of subtle details that weaved into his wake and funeral undeniably was God sent there is no other explanation. We went to pick out a casket, everything looked pretty standard. I walked around the room, looking at the different ones available, nothing stood out, and everything wasn't what I envisioned him to rest in. Then Steve mentioned that he just got an oak casket in, brand new, unused and within our price range. As soon as I saw it, I knew this was not just a coincidence, but sent from above, without a doubt in my mind, I knew this one was for him. The grain of the wood was the same as our kitchen cabinets when I was growing up, even down to the color of the stain. Even people who went through the wake mentioned that the casket fit him perfectly and it was true, he couldn't have made a better one for himself.

My dad was an avid coffee drinker to the point to he would even have coffee at night usually with dessert. When he would make his morning coffee for work and he would add cream and sugar to each individual cup prior to putting it into his thermos. He said it was the only way to make sure that it all tasted the same. I look back and laugh at those little moments because they mean so much more now. Within the last two or three years, my dad's hands began to shake. I remember talking to him on the phone one day and he was saying that it was getting harder to hold the nails while he was working. This was, of course, said during winter in Minnesota so I figured it was the cold or he was being stubborn and not wearing the right gloves or any gloves for that matter so I didn't find it too concerning. However, after the shaking stayed consistent they planned a neurologist appointment after Christmas 2015. I still remember that Christmas and discussing it, stating that I always remember his hands shaking and I played it off as the amount of caffeine that he would drink.

That evening I was about to start dinner in the kitchen, my kids and their dad were home and they were getting the table set. I received a text message from my parents stating that they received news from the neurologist appointment and wanted to Skype. After I read the text message I rolled my eyes, I was about to make dinner and I didn't think it would end up being anything serious. There were times that my stepmother would be overly concerned about symptoms. There were times that she questioned whether or not she would have a type of dementia because she can be rather forgetful. For me, this was just another instance that she has blown out of portion and life would continue on. Honestly, I also didn't want to be bothered, I had food going on the table that was about to get cold and hungry little mouths that needed to be fed.

I was standing next to the garbage can with my hand on the counter when they called. They were both sitting side by side at their dining room table. As soon as I saw their faces my heart sank into the pit of my stomach. They said the neurologist believed it was ALS and suggested that they should go to Mayo Clinic to seek a second opinion. My body was numb; I dropped to the floor and just felt the tears roll down my cheeks. They said they just wanted to let me know even though via Skype was not the way they wanted to tell me, but they said to call them later. The call ended and I just sat there, numb and in shock. My body wouldn't move, I couldn't hear what was going on around me I just knew that life would never be the same.

All the old emotions I had forgotten about and pushed down were coming back up, all the pain that I felt after my mom died, the anxiety, despair, darkness, and sadness. I felt abandoned, broken, left behind and as if there was no one left in the world that cared. I sobbed because for the first time in my life my adoption hit me smack in the chest as if I had the wind knocked out of me. I remember thinking "now I'm really an orphan". The weight and pain of that statement became unbearable; I couldn't even wrap my mind around the concept. Even now I have to distract myself from spiraling down and to remember that I have been loved more deeply by two parents than I ever knew and that I am not alone, I have not been abandoned and I'm not an orphan.

During this time I had mini panic attacks. Moments where I would sob uncontrollably unable to catch my breath with the only thing to keep me grounded with the cool tile of the bathroom floor. Without the help of my kids' dad taking care of them during these moments, I am not sure how I would have handled caring for them as well. He did as best he could to give me the privacy I needed. The pain was consuming, there were moments in the bathroom that I thought I wouldn't be able to stop or even catch my breath. In those moments I would move the rug and try to lay my whole body on the tile, the coolness would somehow keep me grounded.

I knew my thoughts were irrational, I knew I would once again go through the grief cycle that I had become so familiar with. I wasn't ready for this; I was angry, sad and broken all at once. By the age of eight, I had attended at least four funerals, three grandparents and my moms. I don't remember them all but I used to try and make light of it growing up. It was as though I wore it as a badge of honor as if to show off to the world how tough I had it. Deep down I thought that it was bad luck, that everyone around me would eventually leave, and I would be there to grieve and pick up broken pieces of myself all over again.

Knowing that my dad had a terminal illness was one thing, having to tell my child that their Papa was dying was a whole other situation. The questions that filled my mind about how much to tell them, what they should expect and what it means to actually die overwhelmed me. My brain could not process the hundreds of questions that washed over me. When we told the kids, I tried to keep my composure but I felt the tears running down my face. We explained how Papa was sick, that we didn't know how he got sick and that he wasn't going to be able to get better. Explaining such a disease was a challenge in itself, we had to explain how visiting Papa would be different, that they would see Papa sitting down more and needing more help to do things on his own. We answered their questions and off I went back to the bathroom to sob, holding it all together for them was excruciating.

Chapter 3

"Some days the memories still knock the wind out of me" – Unknown

I can still remember this like it was yesterday. It was sunny outside, and we were on the kickball fields at my school in "normal" clothes. Since it was Field Day, we didn't have to wear our uniforms. I had entrusted two friends with a secret crush I had, even though this boy had a girlfriend, a year older and she went to public school. My friends with another girl ran up to me all excited and giggling, as 6th graders typically do. They exclaim "Guess who is single" to me, and all I can remember doing is blankly staring at them since it was completely out of the blue. They continued "Your crush and he wants to go out with you." My heart leaped out of my chest as I exclaimed yes, only to watch in horror as they immediately bent over in laughter. After what seemed like hours of laugher, they uttered it was a joke. I didn't know what to do or even how to respond to that. I never looked at those two girls the same way again.

I was never "that girl". I know you know the type I'm talking about, the popular one with the perfect hair that boys fall over themselves for. To be the girl surrounded by boys who fight for her attention and affections without having to try hard. I have never been that girl, I was the girl who boys were "too good" of friends with to date, the girl that kept her crushes secret because no boy would ever like her the same way, who does not stand out in a crowd, the one that was more on the sidelines then on the field. It took me a long time to be okay with that, to be "one of the guys" instead of a "girly girl". Looking back, I'm glad that I had the friends in high school that I did, those boys were some of the best friends I had.

When I was in a relationship typically I fell hard and I fell fast. Every "love" was "different", but looking back they were all the same. They were all young puppy love. I was looking for someone to just fill the empty void inside without realizing that what I truly needed was to fill my void and heal without someone doing it for me.

I had become emotionally dependent on other people without realizing it. I relied on them to build me up when I was down, to fill me up when I felt empty. I learned that I could not do it alone, that I by myself was not enough. This was my pattern until it completely turned around in college. After one night mixed with too much alcohol with the inability to consent, lack of better judgment on my part and a man who seemed to disregard consent, respect or morals changed me completely.

Each breakup or rejection from a crush was like another blow to my already low self-esteem while adding to my ever growing void. I knew this void existed, however, I struggled into adulthood to understand how to heal from it. In high school, I remember telling my high school sweetheart that I had "walls" for protection and that it was their responsibility to "fill" my void. Being the high school sweetheart of course he said that he would even if it was one shovel full at the time. It is still one of the sweetest things I've been told.

That void became a part of me; it was how I would describe myself throughout high school and college. The void would turn into almost a comfort knowing that it even existed. When I told my high school sweetheart about this void, it was a test he had passed despite me trying to push him away. Eventually, it would become my defense mechanism which would ultimately lead to my destruction.

I never wanted to admit this, but here I am exposing my wounds and scars for the world. This is quite embarrassing; in fact, I just recently started telling people this because I can laugh about it now. In high school, I went on a few tours to different colleges; I wasn't sure where to go. That was until a high school crush mentioned which college he was going too. We were "best friends", we had a few classes together and had hung out together with mutual friends but it never really turned into anything but that. I had the biggest crush on him, thinking about high school now I just sit back and laugh to myself. I shake my head for being so naive and self-conscious, that I had tried to turn myself into someone that he would have a crush on instead of just being me.

Like an impulsive teenager, I followed him to college, he never knew it. I made up other reasons why I chose this college and even believed my own excuses until I would see my crush. We ran into each other from time to time in college, ran into each other at different house parties. He had rejected me throughout high school and college so you would think I would have run in the opposite direction. I saw myself as someone who needed to continue chasing after the wind that I liked the thrill of the chase.

Throughout high school and into college I was intimidating and aggressive as a way to keep everyone out. Even though during those years I was constantly confused as to why I was never asked out on dates. I understand now that it was a defense mechanism because of previous rejection and abandonment. Like a deep seeded root, these rejections and abandonment twisted and turned to create more and more areas in my life to infect. It was more hurtful because at my core I just wanted someone to reach out and care for someone to tell me I'm not crazy and hug me tight. I craved to be nurtured, the little 7 year old inside me was screaming to be heard.

I ran. I ran from problems, relationships, friendships, feelings, heartbreak, and conflict. I stuffed my feelings down into the pit of my stomach hoping they would somehow work themselves out or just disappear. I ran so far I thought I was able to put everything behind me that I would have been fixed and none would be the wiser. I could go about my life continuing to pretend that everything was okay. What I didn't know is that no matter where I ran or where I would try and hide away, my previous hurts continued to twist and turn beneath the surface, like roots growing underneath the ground.

Making friends was always hard while I was pretending to be happy and not show how hurt I was deep down the last thing I wanted to do was befriend other people. It wasn't just romantic relationships that I felt the rejection from; it was from classmates as well. When I was little before starting kindergarten, the friends I played with were typically younger. Those friends were family friends and I don't remember a time when I didn't know them. Once preschool and kindergarten started making friends was hard. My confidence was low and being unsure of yourself doesn't make having friends easier.

My dad used to tell me that I had long legs, I don't think so but he did. Before a piano recital, I was standing in the church with 2 other girls. Their conversation centered on who had the longest legs. Naturally, I inserted myself into the conversation and proudly told them how long my legs were and showed my right leg. My plan had backfired. The two girls looked at each other, looked at me with the most surprised faces turned their heads back toward each other and started giggling. Awkwardly I stood there, watching them laugh and slowly I walked away, and I went looking for someone whom I had already befriended, someone who wouldn't laugh at me.

I have had a handful of friends over the years, ones that I truly trust, that were there for me in a way I needed them to be. Grade school was particularly hard; it seemed that my friends would depend on whose class I was in that year. My circle of friends changed a lot over the years, there are still some that I continue to stay in contact with and others where our contact is over Facebook for birthdays.

I had two “friends” in high school, one I knew since kindergarten and one I had met in middle school through basketball and band. My friendship with them wasn’t really a friendship it was more like a forced friendship because our younger siblings were all in the same class. In high school in between classes, we would stand by our mutual friend’s locker. There was one day, in particular, I walked up to find them giggling and laughing. Of course, I had no idea why they were laughing so I uncomfortably joined in. After this occurred on different occasions, I came to find out that they were laughing at me. Their entertainment before classes was to see if they could get me to join in laughing at myself without even knowing it. This was their entertainment between classes. Great “friends” I surrounded myself huh? Needless to say, I stopped hanging around that group of people; I didn’t want to be around them, much less associate them as friends.

When I was four, I went to an in home daycare, I wasn’t there very long but my experience there is one that I will never forget. From that daycare I only had one friend, he knew me as “Julie with the black hair”. There were several kids that attended but I didn't seem to really befriend any of them.

One day a little girl brought in her pom-poms, everyone was impressed with them. Of course, everyone wanted a turn to shake them. I patiently waited my turn, I didn't know this little girl very well and I was nervous to even ask her. I mustered up all my courage and asked her if I could have a turn. Her response is one that still haunts me; it made me aware for the first time that I was different.

As politely as I could, I asked if I could play with them, she said: "I'm sorry; my mom said that little black girls can't play with them." That conversation has been forever seared in my brain. I don't remember my reaction just the feelings of absolute rejection and hurt. I knew I wasn't black, I was Korean. After that, I didn't ask to play with her or her toys again. I isolated myself from the other kids, except for the girl that bullied me, her I was unable to avoid.

Thankfully I have found real friends, but it doesn't make the anxiety go away. Even now in the very back of my mind, there is a little voice inside me that tells me my friends aren't really my friends. I have to hold back the urge to ask them if they are mad at me or if we are okay. I have no reason not to trust them; in fact, they have been there for me through so much over the years. They have been nothing but genuine friends and yet in the back of my mind each time we hang out I end up being self-conscious of all my actions.

Chapter 4

"There is only one way to avoid criticism: do nothing, say nothing and be nothing." - Aristotle

I have always been very sensitive and my feelings can be easily hurt, particularly by those closest to me. Sometimes all it would take is a look and I would feel something wrong in my gut. If that happened you could bet that I would be walking on eggshells with hurt feelings to try and not have that feeling repeat itself. As the years continued, I pushed down all the hurt feelings, rejections, and pain. I thought it was for protection or that I could somehow pretend they weren't beneath the surface growing and twisting like an ever present weed. Later in my adult life, I learned that the only one hurting with those walls up was me. I had built these walls to see who loved me enough to knock them down but instead, it kept out the very thing I longed for.

I used to say that I was always the one getting my heartbroken that guys were always the one breaking up with me but in reality, I had become very good at pushing others away. I had gone through so much rejection and conflict throughout middle school and high school that it was just easier to be hurt and stay isolated then to subject myself to more pain. Looking back, I realized even then that I would "ruin any chance at happiness". I had let all the roots take over my life and unknowingly kept myself isolated and hurting. Part of me knew these roots had taken over, that my life had become something I couldn't control, but I didn't know how to stop it, I didn't know what I needed. It just seemed like my poor flower bed that I would be taken over and consumed by these weeds.

After years of constant criticism and negative feedback, I lived in a constant state of not being content and confident in my own skin. That I was somehow had managed to consistently disappoint those around me. No matter what I achieved or how passive and agreeable I was, it would never be enough. There was always something wrong, there was always something to do better or someone else to be like. I learned that my worth was conditional, that I would have to act a certain way or do something significant to stop the criticism. It wore me down, I became less and less sure of who I was. No longer was I comfortable in my own skin, I had to change who I was in order to "fit in" because just being me wasn't enough.

When you ask people to describe me, they may say that I am outgoing, strong, sure of myself and confident. During this time in my life, that is not how I felt, it was just the way I acted. I had learned to ignore the ever growing weed inside me. I used a mask to hide everything going on inside, I learned to act confident, outgoing and sure of myself. It was easy to pretend to be something I wasn't. I kept the knotted up weed hidden away from the world so people would not be aware of how hurt I was.

If something negative was said about me, my immediate thought was "well it must be true" or I would immediately start defending myself. I was always on the defensive, I needed to feel heard and understood. Each interaction I had with people I would already have an explanation or excuse ready in case it would be immediately needed. I eventually learned not to accept compliments or encouraging words because it had become a habit to defend myself and take each statement as criticism. In my longest relationship, I would eventually discover that the compliments stopped because I would negate each compliment, further hurting myself. He said that it would cut his ego and make him not want to compliment me since I didn't believe his words were true.

It has taken me a very long time to accept a compliment, even now sometimes I have to bite my tongue. This root runs deep, I know it will take practice and time to completely eradicate this from my habits but I will keep pulling out this root.

After my mom died things obviously changed around our house, my dad would spend evenings in his office working after I went to bed. My uncles and family friends seemed to help out a lot by bringing me to piano lessons or gymnastics and just helping out in general. There was one night while we were sitting at the dinner table and I was poking at my food. My dad asked me what was wrong, I hung my head and whispered that I missed mom as I tried to hold back tears. That is one of the only times that I can recall that we just sat and cried together at the dinner table. I'm sure there were more instances but this one sticks out in my mind. I needed him, to comfort me, to just give me a hug and squeeze me tight. I cannot imagine what he must have been going through but I know I just needed my dad. I needed to know he missed her too, that I was not the only one whose world had changed or fallen apart. I can't imagine the grief or sadness he was experiencing, but I felt lonely and confused.

I don't remember having a lot of talks with my dad surrounding my mom's death. I remember the long nights he would spend in his office working. I would walk down the stairs peek into his office and tell him that I couldn't sleep, that I needed to fall asleep in his bed. There wasn't another reason except I was lonely and somehow sleeping on my mom's side was a comfort. There were many nights spent falling asleep to Cheers and Seinfeld. I needed the emotional nurturing from him, something that I craved. I don't know everything he was going through at the time; I know that even now I can't imagine how he must have felt. All I know is that I needed him to be emotionally there for me and he wasn't and by doing so unintentionally had me pining for emotionally unavailable men later in life. I don't blame him at all, I know that he was doing the best that he knew how with the resources given to him.

Growing up my life was surrounded by criticism and comparison. I grew up in a family that believed that if they looked good on the outside then clearly things were good on the inside. Conversations at dinner were filled with who had gotten a new job, how much people were making, statements that started with "why can't you be more like..." Throughout high school, college and even now, conversations are typically around someone's new house, how much it cost, someone's new job, how much they are making an hour, who just got engaged, how helpful other people's children are and the list continues on and on. It is not just from immediate family but extended family as well. After years of hearing that those statements, it seemed that no matter what I did it would never be good enough, that *I* was never going to be good enough. It felt like constant rejection as no matter what I did someone else's son or daughter would be five steps ahead and I would constantly hold up the end of the line. It took a very long time and a lot of encouraging words for me to let those comments roll of my back. Now I know that I am not racing anyone but myself, that I am unlike anyone else and keeping up with everyone else doesn't have to be my path.

I learned from a young age not to speak up, to keep my opinions to myself and to just "go along to get along". This would make things better, my dad would remind me to just go with the flow, even if I was uncomfortable or I disagreed with something. There was always a mention of just do this for me or can't you just suck it up. Even as an adult I would listen to my stepmother going on one of her rants and my dad would just look at me and go “just let her talk”, he would roll his eyes about something or just make another passive comment. Too many times I was given the instruction to just sit there and listen to someone gripe about this and that because they cared. Very often I would find myself having conversations with my dad over the phone and he would just continue to excuse the behavior saying that my stepmother liked to talk and it would be in my best interest to continue to let her.

Growing up there was always something to be criticized about, whether it was how clean my room was, whether a shirt was wrinkled or not if the “right” clothes were on, why I wasn’t friends with certain people or found certain boys attractive, anything really. It seemed more important to “keep up with the Jones’” then it was anything else.

I remember conversations about what type of clothes were appropriate to go to church in or how they couldn’t believe what so-and-so was wearing in church, sometimes it even got to the point discussing who was *in* church. It was exhausting even now talking about it makes me tired and annoyed. It pushed me away from church for a long time; I didn’t like the church I grew up in. It always seemed like who was there was more important than why we were there. I used to find every excuse for why I didn’t go to church in college. I was so thankful when I started working and when my days to work fell on church days.

If you were to ask my stepmother, to this day she would probably explain that my behaviors and attitudes are due to the fact that I harbor animosity towards her. In doing so these behaviors and attitudes were to "punish" my dad, this was her explanation for why I did not call every day, stay on the phone for an hour or want to discuss the happenings of the small town I grew up in.

My stepmother would most likely discuss me to anyone who will listen that I intentionally punish her for "taking my mom's place" and that I could be one of the most selfish people because I only think about myself. How dare I think of my immediate family, my kids first? How dare I try to ensure my job is secure so I have money to visit? How dare I have a life that does not circle around small town middle America and my extended family? How dare I not engage in the ongoing circus of gossiping and comparing other's achievements to my own? How dare I don't care for people whom I haven't spoken to since high school or what is going on in their life. How dare I have a life that is separate from them?

After I had my son the criticism took a drastic shift and the focus was now centered on him. My parents seemed to have an opinion on everything, from baptism to extracurricular activities; their intrusive comments filled most of our conversations. In 2014, my parents decided to drive down and surprise my son and me for our birthdays. While we were sitting in the parking lot I received a text message from my dad, it was a picture of him standing by a sign saying “Welcome to Kentucky”. Tears filled my eyes, I was so excited. The weekend of their visit would be a birthday I will never forget.

During the day my parents kept both of our kids while we went off to work. While they were getting my son ready, a comment about his jeans, how short they were and how the majority of his clothes were from second hand stores. Even with several conversations about this issue before, it still managed to be a point of criticism for my parents. After dinner both my dad and stepmother started discussing how our son needed new clothes, his jeans were too short and how we could live with ourselves because we allowed him to go around dressed like that.

By this time I was fed up, it was my birthday. I told them the same answer I would tell them every time this topic was brought up. Our son would grow out of clothes so fast that it was cheaper to buy second hand clothes then brand new ones every couple of months. The jeans that were too short were the only pair in his drawer that was too short. Neither of us had an issue with buying him second hand clothes, especially because most of them still looked brand new. Answering their comments in this way only created another argument, I didn’t want to argue, I wasn’t going to understand their point of view and they clearly weren’t going to understand mine.

My emotions were sky high and my frustration had gotten the best of me, so I stormed into the master bedroom and locked myself in the closet.

It was dark in there and I could drown out the arguing with socks pressed against my ears. Two hours later, after my boyfriend had spent the majority of that time standing up for me all three of them came into the bedroom. Hell could have frozen over after what came out of my parents' mouths. They apologized for their comments and then followed it up with the word "but". No good apology ever has the word "but" in it, it negates the apology. Their sentences continued with more criticism about what I'm not even sure anymore.

It was after this interaction that my boyfriend finally understood. He had witnessed firsthand the level of criticism that I grew up with. His words of comfort and understanding meant so much. No longer did I feel like I had made things like this up in my head, someone finally understood.

Chapter 5

"They burned the bridge and then ask why you don't visit." - Unknown

The summer of 2016, I was picking up my son from spending two weeks with his grandparents. Since my dad continued to battle ALS there were additional people going along for their 8 hour road trip. Not only were my dad and stepmother in the car, but my two aunts and my uncle. Auntie lives out in California; I hadn't seen her for at least a year.

After I had driven over eight hours through two different severe thunderstorm warnings/tornado watches, the first thing out of her mouth isn't a hello or a nice to see you; instead, I am met with immediate criticism about completing "such a long drive alone". This was not the first time nor the last that I have made this drive, in fact, there were several times that I had driven this before and never once has she had an opinion about my safety or length of the trip. It wasn't until now that she seemed all concerned about how far I had driven alone. My response was rather curt and I mentioned something like I've completed the drive before, it's not that long, I enjoy the drive, whatever I could come up with that wasn't snarky because I just wanted to see my son and my dad.

My initial instinct was to be snarky, to immediately retaliate with hurtful words and begin an argument, but this time I wouldn't succumb to her level. If I would have a little more extra money, I would have immediately picked up my son and turned around to start the 12 hour drive back to the South. I wanted to spend the extra with my dad and sometimes it was a hard decision to keep my mental health and see him at the same time. I always wanted to spend time with him, but now it would be more difficult since there were so many extra people to help him.

You may think I'm being overly sensitive, that I need to have thick skin, I've heard it all before. However, I can tell you that after a childhood and lifetime of this constant negative feedback it isn't as easy to let the comments roll off your back. The comments start to wear you down like weights continuously being added to your back eventually after enough weight you break. Years and years of these comments my thick skin was no longer thick and every little comment felt like a razor blade. Life as I knew it was nothing more than criticisms and feedback.

Growing up I remember how these aunts obsessed over their looks from their perfectly ironed pants, hair sprayed hair and perfectly colored lipstick. The routine they had getting ready for the day included showering, makeup, hair, and freshly pressed clothes. I don't remember a time that no makeup or a simple t-shirt was acceptable attire. After my mom passed these two would ensure that I looked my best during special occasions, specifically my first communion. As the years went on my relationship with them would drastically change. It seems I have already been isolated from them and rest of my extended family. This all occurred because I continued to fail to their expectations while they cut off their communication with me. I'm sure you're wondering what my offense was to cause such discrimination.

As I have said before, I began grieving over my dad's terminal illness from the day I was told of his diagnosis. I probably did not handle it the best way and isolated myself which included taking a break from constant interaction and interrogation with my parents to focus on me with therapy. Even now, knowing there is a possibility that they will read everything I have written, I can just imagine the conversations going on behind my back as I type. This is how it seems my dad's family communicates, to discuss people behind their backs without investigation, something that I had grown to be accustomed too.

I can read the intrusive inappropriate guilt tripping text messages, which wouldn't be the first time I've received them. I can also hear the nasty name calling voicemails that have yet to be left, another thing I have been accustomed too. I have been unapologetically truthful; too many years have gone by with these comments hiding in the dark. It is time someone shines the light into those dark spaces.

It wasn't until quite recently that I have really seen them for who they are. Their constant criticism is demanding and exhausting. It typically begins with polite suggestions, why don't you do this, what about doing this, oh no they aren't clean enough, here let me show you how to do this correctly and then it moves onto the guilt. Oh, the guilt trips I have heard throughout my life. If something did not live up to someone's expectations, then there was someone who had been disappointed or someone else's child you weren't as good as.

After my dad's funeral, Auntie texted me suggesting that she wondered where the sweet little girl was that I had been growing up. To which she implied that little girl doesn't exist anymore. This was after she proceeded to tell me how wrong I was for blaming my stepmother for my dad's death. Her text message included statements that I had never uttered out loud, things that I had only mentioned to my therapist and cousin via text. The only way Auntie or anyone else would have gotten these details would be if she took my cell phone and read through my text messages. This wouldn't be the first time my privacy had been violated, it is not unheard of for anyone, including immediate family members to go through my journal, car or listen to my phone calls.

While at the luncheon following my dad's funeral my kids' dad and his mother gave me a card. They told me that this card was specifically for me and that they were giving another one to the rest of my immediate family, stating that I would understand as soon as I opened my card. I concealed this card in my purse and waited until I was no longer surrounded by family to open it. Inside I understood there was money inside with kind words written by the two of them. To ensure that no one else would see this card, I left it in my car on the passenger seat with my car doors locked. The following morning, I packed up my car and headed to meet my kids, their dad and his mother so we could start the drive back to South Carolina.

I pulled up to the house that they were staying at, after talking to them, I find out that my stepmother called his mom to find out about the money that was in my card, and mentioned what was written in the card. My stepmother had covertly disguised it as making sure that the money was specifically for me. The evening before when I saw her, there was no mention of the card, and I didn't notice anything out of the ordinary in my car the following morning. At some point in the night, someone went into my card, read through the cards I had left in there and looked in the envelopes. After years of this type of intrusion, I should have known better and taken more precautions to ensure the card was well hidden. That was the furthest thing from my mind; the thought didn't even dawn on me that my family would go as far as to go through my car. Looking back I should have realized

To set the record straight, because I feel that this needs to be aired out. To the best of my knowledge I have not blamed my stepmother for my dad's death or even the disease. What was communicated after he left this earth was that there concern because his bipap machine was taken off, and somehow it was thought that having it off may have progressed things faster. I knew there was no way to know if something like that would have impacted the progression of the disease. Auntie was even part of that conversation, in fact, several family members were part of that conversation, and I don't remember saying that I blamed anyone.

When the guilt trips started it was all surrounded around who were you disappointing or letting down or who's child you weren't acting like. If I wasn't disappointing one parent then it was the other and if it wasn't them there would be someone else to disappoint. If after all the different ways to guilt trip didn't work then it would escalate into passive aggressive comments while tattling to other family members. After the tattling came to the exact same cycle from those family members. Typically it would be my stepmother calling and to tell me that the following criticism wasn't from her but it was from my dad, that he said these things she was relaying. There are a few instances in which my dad and I would discuss these types of things, and if we did it was rather brief.

In the world of freshly pressed linens, sparkling clean floors and starched shirts, I am the stubborn stain that refuses to lift. My room or apartment never had to be absolutely sparkling clean all of the time. I would be reminded by this when my family would visit places I lived. Sitting there displayed on my kitchen counter more than once was a bucket or even a glass filled with dirty water. The dirty water was from my floors being washed while I was at work.

I never really fit into the mold; I never really wanted to be a part of "their world". My life didn't revolve around my small town or people I knew from grade school, high school or their siblings. There was a whole world outside of the fishbowl and I desperately wanted to find my place in it. There was always something that needed to be corrected, perfection was the only option and even then there would be something to criticize.

Anything that could be misconstrued into insubordination could be treated as if they were "less than" or were somehow disappointing a family member. If your room was picked up, vacuumed and dusted, that was criticized, if you didn't help your parents out enough with the task at hand, that was disappointing or if you didn't have a sparkling clean house during family gathers. It may even go as far as restricting family members with younger child during get the holidays due to the possibility of a mess or stain on white furniture.

This is not to imply that I don't like a "clean" home. However cleanliness standards typically vary from person to person but to have a home that consistently appears like a floor model without appearing "lived" in would be where my line is drawn. The places I have lived looked lived in and though I may not always dust each nook and cranny but at the bare minimum my home is picked up.

Aside from the criticism, it appeared my stepmother thought that spending holidays and buying Christmas presents for my cousins on my mom's side was getting "too extended". The conversation she had with my dad was about buying gifts for my cousin's children. My stepmother implied that it was gotten "too far out" on that side of the family to continue to buy gifts for everyone. It seemed as if my connection to them and my mom was in jeopardy. In the beginning, since I was so young, I really did not have any control nor did I really understand everything going on around me. Spending time with them seemed to become almost burdensome for her, it was if their presence made it difficult for her, as if their presence was a constant reminder of my mom, which was something I needed, someone to remember her and tell me all about her. While I was growing up through middle school, high school and especially college, spending time with my mom's side of the family seemed more like an item to check off a list. They were still family to me, and they still saw me and my dad as a family. Trying to understand another perspective seemed to be too complicated for me to figure out. It felt as if she was trying to eradicate my mom's side of the family. If we were able to spend time with my mom's family, the time was limited and part of me seemed as if it felt forced. It would take years until I would fully understand the magnitude of this.

My cousin died in a tragic motorcycle accident just after I had made it through the first trimester during my son's pregnancy. This was not something I had shared yet with my entire family and I knew that at my cousin's funeral was not at the right time. At the funeral I remember wearing a skirt, I had to make sure that it hid the fact that I was starting to show and had to act as normal as possible. Hiding such a thing was extremely difficult for me, I wanted to tell them, even though I wasn't married and this had happened out of the blue, it was still something I felt needed to be told. During the funeral, I remember trying to avoid any sort of eye contact or interaction with my uncles, aunts, and cousins. I felt too ashamed to try and look them in the eye. My secret ate away at me; it wasn't until several weeks later that I emailed them. My nerves had been shot after telling my parents and my boyfriend's parents. Knowing that I had let down another family member was unbearable. Just the thought of having to tell them made my already weak stomach get twisted into knots.

I barely knew my cousin; it had been years since we had spent a significant time together. I had spent time with him growing up, but over the years and with the limited time we spent with my mom's family, I lost touch with him. We grew up and being that he was older, he was starting to date women, eventually got married and had started growing his family. My mom's family didn't know I was pregnant at the time; I hadn't had the opportunity to tell them yet. I didn't know how to tell them. After years of limited contact, they seemed like strangers to me instead of part of my family. They were the only connection left to my mom that I so deeply needed, by this time there were only bits and pieces I remember. I had forgotten the sound of her voice and her infectious laugh everyone would talk about. The only family of hers that remained was her brothers and my cousins. My dad didn't really discuss my mom, and if he did it was just about how he missed her or how much she loved me, the conversations rarely went any further than that. Trying to get him to talk any further about her seemed to just add strain to my relationship with my stepmother.

I didn't really know my mom. What I knew, I knew only because it was things I had been told or the few things I remember. Even now, remembering her is a struggle; in my mind I still see the woman hooked up to IVs and oxygen tubing. That is not how I want to remember my mom; I wanted to remember her unforgettable laugh and her passion for teaching. I wish I knew more, I barely know anything about her and trying to get any information was like pulling teeth with my dad. Thankfully as the years have passed, I have reconnected with my mom's family and have had the opportunity to hear some stories about her younger years and read her high school commencement speech.

Years of hearing all the criticism and constantly being reminded to be passive, to let people talk in order to get along, had become my habit. This is how I learned to address conflict, to just pretend as if nothing happened and to continue moving forward. Even now, another cousin, Cuz barely says a word to me. Only being a month apart in age and being very close when we were growing up and through college, I don't recall him reaching out to me after I moved down South. It seemed I always reached out to him. With the news of my dad's diagnosis, I thought for sure that he would reach out or at the very least say something, anything. Reaching out never came; I reached out again to him in which he offered very little support. I was considered selfish because I wanted to discuss my feelings because I should have put my sole focus on my dad and disregarded any feelings I was dealing with.

Even at my dad's funeral, Cuz didn't say more than a few words to me and when he did it was because I initiated it, I don't recall a goodbye or anything. I can only imagine what has been said or continues to be said about me to my family members. It saddens me to know that instead of reaching out to me and having a mature conversation, my decisions, actions and behavior are potentially discussed behind my back and based off of other people's opinions or observations.

The trip to pick up my son was the most amusing; thankfully it is something I can laugh about. My goal the entire trip would be to minimize and defuse any and all conflict that would ensue. I was prepared for criticism, snide passive aggressive comments, and intrusive questions from my stepmother and aunts. I had to remind myself that I was there for my son and to spend a little time with my dad. We all stayed in a two bedroom suite, my son, me, my uncle, my two aunts, my dad and stepmother. It was the smallest space we have ever all been confined to that I could remember. Almost immediately their comments started, first it was because I drove such a distance alone, when it wasn't that it was because I didn't shower that morning, or wasn't going to shower that night, the fact I didn't rinse out a "dirty" glass from the cupboard before pouring myself a glass of wine or my worst offense yet, spending one on one time with my uncle.

If it wasn't my aunts asking him questions including what we talked about on the way to and from the lobby for coffee, it was someone else wanting to know everything I said or what I said about her or my aunts. My aunts seemed to be jealous that my uncle and I had spent some time one on one.

This trip was the first time I can recall them criticizing someone other than me. My uncle was berated by my aunts because he only brought a toiletries kit, a change of shirt and clean underwear. He didn't think to bring an "overnight bag", that itself seemed like a tragedy that he had to carry his extra set of clothes and a toiletries kit in a miscellaneous bag. I wish I was making this up but there was a serious discussion on why an overnight bag was needed and by discussion I mean my aunts talking at my uncle. How he survived in the car for over 7 hours with them, two days in a row I will never know.

A couple weeks after that trip, I received a letter in the mail, from my other uncle (OU). The man is sixty years old and writes me a letter; I cannot recall a legitimate conversation with this man in who knows how long. Typically you can't have a serious discussion with him; it ends up being more jokes and gossip than anything. The first sentence of his letter reads "Drake is a great guy: too bad you and (my son's dad) are so fucked up - poor Drake".

You read that correctly. Because my life is not how they wanted it to turn out or because I am not married to the father of my children, I am fucked up. This is not the first time my OU called me fucked up. The first was about a year ago the summer after my dad was diagnosed with ALS. That time I was fucked up because I did not call every single day and no one would ever act like that unless they were on drugs so therefore I must clearly be on drugs.

This letter was four pages long; it talked about how I must clearly be on drugs because I am so selfish that I don't come take care of my dad because I owe him that much for providing such a wonderful life. That I need to grow up because I still harbor "anger" towards my stepmother and are therefore taking it out on my dad and I need to "get over myself". My favorite was that I "pissed away" college. As if grieving over my dad's terminal illness wasn't enough, I was now being rejected by the very family I grew up around. This uncle would take care of me when my dad couldn't. He would bring me to piano lesson, watch me at his house and just spend time with me. His letter continued about how I don't talk to him. Damn, can you blame me? Who would want to someone that jumps to conclusions and calls you fucked up and on drugs? That letter sent me into a panic attack, the first I had in months.

Don't misunderstand, I am very grateful to my parents, particularly my dad for making sure I was involved in sports and other extracurricular activities. OU even helped out bringing me to and from activities from time to time. My aunts always made sure that I looked picture perfect for special occasions. It is because of this that their hurtful words affected me as deeply as they did. Am I thankful I had such supportive and involved parents? I am. By no means do I think I lacked any sort of support while growing up. I also fully admit that I had a wonderful childhood and was provided with more opportunities and support from my parents.

However, as a parent, I also see that some of that goes with just being a parent. My children are in elementary school and they want to be involved in so many different activities and want to do so many different things, of course, I am going to make sure they are involved. That is what being a parent does, I don't expect them to "pay me back" when they are adults because I made sure they were involved in things. My kids don't owe me anything for being their cook, nurse, house cleaner, driving service or a homework helper. I am raising human beings, this isn't a paid job, and they are MY responsibility. What kind of parents parent for the "credit" after the fact or even the type of parents that need to be "paid back" for being a parent? I don't want to raise my children in a home where they think they owe me something, they are my children and like the giving tree, they can leave me as a stump.

It is amazing how different people act when you face them in person. While I was back with my family toward the end of my dad's fight, these family members all of a sudden became like the family I remember growing up. Of course the passive aggressive comments, polite snide suggestions were ever present but for a split second, I stopped feeling like everyone's emotional punching bag. For once in my adult life something was more important than how everything appeared, what mattered was being there for my dad.

Chapter 6

"We sabotage the great things in our life because deep down we don't feel worthy of having the great things" - Taressa Riazzi

By college, I had become a full blown abandoholic. Yes, you read that correctly, I didn't say alcoholic, I said abandoholic. By this time in my life, I had become a master at abandoning and self-sabotaging relationships. A few months would pass or just a date or two with a man and I would find a reason why they weren't my type. I had a variety of excuses from the type of their favorite car, their name (yes this was an actual reason), I still had feelings for an ex or no butterflies, and there were numerous others that were used over my years in college.

Because of all this, I earned the nickname "Black Widow." Along the way I ended up breaking hearts, ruining friendships and centered my world on getting my next attention fix. When I would look around the grass was constantly greener on the other side, and I would sprint to get there. There was always someone else who gave me attention and I would move on and go get the next attention fix. It was like a drug, the attention was intoxicating. Unknowingly becoming the one thing I used to make fun of.

My social life in college would be to ensure I had my attention fix. There would be instances when I would have little to no interest in these men and I would continue talking with them because it was added attention or just someone to flirt with. Eventually, that would come back to haunt me.

After sabotaging a seven month relationship, I continued to chase after my unattainable crush, my college sweetheart, someone who was emotionally unavailable. We had instant chemistry but he continued his long distance relationship, stating that there was never a good time to end it. Early that summer he finally broke up with her and my first initial thought was that we would finally have a chance to start a relationship but I was wrong. Once he was single, he wanted to truly be single, to go and date other women yet he continued to spend time with me and act as though we were together, or so I thought. One evening there was a group of us that went out to one of the bars I frequented in college, he had a fraternity brother that was a bartender there.

Due to my abandaholic nature, I had recently agreed to go on a date with a man from another fraternity, Mister; if we weren't in a relationship then I would continue to keep my options open. I always had an escape plan. We had flirted some but never had really hung out together. This night at the bar would be one of the lowest points while in college.

There was a bus that would pick people up across the street from the fraternity I was living in for the summer. It would take us downtown to the bars, so there was a group of us that went to go visit their fraternity brother who was bartending.

There were a few new people hanging out with that group, one of which caught the attention of my crush. Like any single guy he spent most of the evening giving her all of his attention, of course, I was hurt, I had that thought we were going to start a relationship. I started to complain to the bartender who ended up handing me a couple of shots and a drink or two. Well, things start to get a little hazy after that. I remember that I just wanted the hurt to go away and then I saw my crush and the other girl making out on the dance floor.

My heart sank into my toes and like any classic abandaholic; I immediately reached out to Mister. Without a doubt, in my mind, I knew I would get the attention I needed and the distraction from the pain.

He is a member of a fraternity and someone whom I would rather forget I've had any interaction with. Prior to this specific evening, I met Mister during Sweetheart week at his fraternity; he had also taken me to their Sweetheart dance. Initially, he was nice, typical college man, nothing that stood out or really made him memorable. After losing the sweetheart competition we didn't really hang out until several months to a year later during one of their house parties. He had asked for my number, at the time I wasn't sure about him either way, I wasn't overly interested but was not interested at the same time. He was studying law and seemed to be a nice guy. He asked me out on a date to the movies and of course, I accepted, I wanted to go to the movies but also wanted to get to know him better.

Well the evening that my crush hurt me when I saw him kissing another girl, in my hurt and intoxicated state, I knew I had to leave the bar. With an empty purse and several hours, until the party bus returned, and all my friends wanting to stay at the bar, I did the one thing I knew would get me back to campus.

After closing my eyes a couple of times and trying to see who exactly I was texting, I sent Mister a text message asking if he would be able to come and pick me up. His response was a red flag, one that I should have picked up on, but I was drunk, hurt and just wanted to get back to my bed. He replied back stating he was about to leave downtown but wanted to know what was in it for him. Looking back I should have ended the conversation there and found someone else, even though with my state of mind I couldn't think of anyone else. I responded that he would be able to get a goodnight kiss, nothing more. He agreed and within minutes I remember getting into his white car.

The details following me getting into the car are hard to recall. Due to the amount of alcohol I consumed the details are rather quite unclear, however, I am sure of the following. As he drove back to campus, he stated that he wasn't drinking that night and was headed to a house party. He asked if I wanted to join. Of course, I wanted too, it would be a great distraction from the hurt I was still feeling. The conversation continued and the only thing I remember was him mentioning he needed to stop at his house, grab something to drink and we would go to the house party.

Next thing I am aware of I say hi to his roommate and we end up kissing in his room, he tells me that he has had a crush on me since sweetheart week. The word no never uttered from my lips, but I also do not recall anything about the rest of the night except seeing a condom and walking into the fraternity I was staying at.

The following morning I woke up numb with the smell of someone else's sweat on me. I can still smell the stench of body odor and immediately I become nauseated. I woke up feeling disgusted; a shower couldn't remove how dirty I felt on the inside. Completely confused, hung over and unsure of what happened I called into work sick that day. News of what had happened had already spread through the fraternities. Mister's fraternity house was next door to the one I was living at that summer. Apparently, after being dropped off at the house, I was staying at he ran around both fraternities boasting about how he had finally nailed the Asian.

I was mortified and disgusted. Shortly after that my crush came into my room, said a few nasty things only for me to find out moments later he had the other girl in his room, she had stayed the night. Out of frustration, guilt, pain, and embarrassment, I kicked my couch. My abandonment issues had gotten the best of me and the only way I knew how to cope was to kick something. Obviously, I wasn't aware of the consequences of my actions even though I knew my foot would be injured. My toes never healed right, I never went to the doctor, and I just used ice and limped around until it didn't hurt to limp anymore. My right foot was bruised as was my ego and my heart.

Looking back I probably should have filed charges; I had friends tell me that I should have. Listening to them wasn't the easiest because I knew I had too much to drink and I knew that I had already mentioned kissing him, but it went too far, *he* had taken it too far. He didn't even have a drink that night and there I was barely able to walk straight and probably slurring my speech.

I ran in the opposite direction after that. I tried to tuck that interaction away in the furthest part away from my feelings and mind. The subject was not to be discussed and even when I bring it up now I just give people enough information to figure out what happened. It changed my perspective on men; no longer did I want the attention, especially from those that reminded me of him. It was the last thing I wanted. I hardened my heart even more and went full on into protection mode. Even now I cringe if someone reminds me of him, I can feel my body tense up and I immediately want scream and run out of the room, it makes my skin crawl.

I had learned throughout middle school and high school that it was much easier to protect myself from getting hurt if I just let the boys like me and then leave them or self-sabotage so I would fulfill my own irrational thought, that I would be abandoned again.

I never knew that I was my own self-fulfilling fear, that I was causing all this pain to me thinking it was out of protection... I was my own worst enemy. I wanted so badly to be chased after by the opposite sex and to be loved, but at the same time, I didn't want to get rejected or abandoned. It was a vicious cycle; I wanted to be close to someone but the fear of them leaving was so much greater that I would self-sabotage. I would attach myself to these men quickly believing my soul mate had arrived. Then something would happen, I would immediately lose interest and start looking for my "actual" soul mate. I believe that once my soul mate came along, everything else would immediately fit into place, which I would be created wholly by this other person.

I wanted to run away starting in middle school and start with a clean slate somewhere else. At one point I even looked into emancipation to get out of my house. I was truly unhappy and depressed. When high school came around I dreamed of going out of state, of getting out of the small fishbowl of a town that I lived in. Initially, my dream was to live in California and be at the beach all day. The beach is one of the few places I truly feel at peace. My dream of attending an out of state school was quickly dashed by Auntie who lives in California. All she could talk about is how expensive everything was and how difficult it was being so far away from family. That is what I wanted, to be as far away as humanly possible from the toxicity, the judgment, the criticism, and the facade that everything was going well. I didn't move out of state until after college and it wasn't to California like I had hoped. I ended up moving about 1,100 miles away to South Carolina. It was the best decision I ever made.

I am passive by nature, something I unintentionally picked up from my dad. I don't like conflicts and even worse, I hate feeling like my relationship with someone is going through a rough patch. At times it would feel as if I was walking on eggshells because I didn't want to start a conflict, as I was unsure how to navigate it without screaming and crying. I struggle with poor communication skills, I didn't know how to fight in a healthy way nor did I know how to effectively communicate my wants and needs. Not the best combination when your decade long relationship is rocky from its foundation up and you are unaware of how to address your concerns.

My pattern was to "immediately" want love and then to self-sabotage. I believed in love at first sight, the over the top romantic stories and grandiose gestures. Fairy tales seemed possible, that once the one was with me everything would be perfect. Love would be all we needed. Yet on the flip side, I thought I was too dark and twisted to love, that because of everything that had happened to me that I was not good enough to be unconditionally loved. It is this constant longing of wanting something so badly but fearing in the very back of your heart and mind that you will end up unhappy and alone.

I had created my own world of unhappiness that I desperately wanted to get out of but I had become accustomed to it. It was safe. It was a life I knew, a life I knew how to control and exist in. Everything else seems unattainable I saw what I wanted but I didn't know how to get there, especially since I had gotten so much resistance from my parents.

Towards the end of my college years, I finally thought I had given up my abandaholic behavior. Thinking that enough time had passed that everything was in the past and wouldn't affect my future. By this time I thought that I had found that someone who would love me despite my flaws, my scars and my cart full of emotional baggage, which I continued to ignore even, existed. I had convinced myself that I was well adjusted and had no underlying issues to work out or confront. I played the part well. At times I even fooled myself.

Since that summer or fall, I started officially dating my crush. One evening, he went out for a "guys" night, I spending some time with some other friends of mine. Several hours into the evening I began to receive text messages and phone calls from friends that my boyfriend is making out at the bar with another woman. Furiously I called him screamed something nasty and immediately hang up the phone. It wasn't the first time this boy had hurt me in such a way, and there I was again rejected and abandoned. Over the years I let that hurt fester inside; it slowly began to poison me. Over the years I would continue to hold this over his head almost during every argument this incident would be brought up over and over. I thought I had healed from that wound, but I had just put a band aid on it and went back to ignoring there was ever a problem between us.

The last serious relationship, with my college sweetheart, was likely one of the most inconsistent relationships to my knowledge. It started out when we were in college, both dating other people at the time. We met once in my sophomore year and then didn't hang out again until several months later. It wasn't until the spring of my junior year that an attraction even developed despite us being in long distance relationships.

Of course, the abandoholic and self sabotager inside me wanted instant gratification, the chance at "immediate" love and the constant attention at the time was more appealing than a long distance love. Like any woman with abandonment issues, I ran and I sabotaged the long distance relationship, broke another heart and went chasing after someone who was emotionally unavailable. The abandaholic inside me figured that this man would be the one, not the last one or the last serious relationship before that. I had created my own fantasy that we would start dating and everything would just magically fall into place. None of that was our reality, we would spend the next couple of years of hurting each other in an on again off again relationship.

The first few years we were in South Carolina were hard. They were hard because we weren't around family or friends; it was just us in a new state with a baby on the way and only one of us having a job. We barely knew anyone. We met people through a coworker of my boyfriend these people were essentially her friends and we just tagged along because we were new in town. It wasn't the same at first, but it beat being alone. We missed our friends, more importantly, I missed my friends. With all the overstepping of boundaries that my family had, my friends were my lifeline. My friends had become my family, the women became the sisters I never had, and the men, the older overprotective brothers I always wished for. I hated being far away from them but it felt so good to be away from all the other toxicity. I finally felt like I could breathe without someone watching over my shoulder.

With this newfound distance and freedom, came a lot more uncertainty, more weeds that would start to crawl beneath the surface. The first year we didn't live together, he had his "bachelor pad" and I had an apartment for me and our son. We spent most nights together but he still had his place, he was able to escape from all the responsibilities that a newborn required if he needed the extra sleep. At the time I wasn't working, he was providing for us so like I had previously done; I went along to get along. I never mentioned how hurt I felt or how I just needed him there. Eventually, I would come to believe the lie that he didn't care about me, that I was just the caretaker of our son and I was more useful to him as that than as his girlfriend.

We didn't have a lot of babysitters so either we had to divide and conquer, meaning we would split up to get more errands ran or chores done around our apartment. However, that put a lot of stress on me, I was alone most of the time. He had found a few hobbies that he was passionate about, which would lead to him going away for the weekend or needed to sleep in because he was out late the night before. I didn't have a lot of friends or activities I was involved in so I felt left out, tired and used. I didn't want to miss out on life, I felt excluded from this man whom I moved to the Southeast and started raising a son together. I thought we had a life together, that we were a team but I was left feeling alone, unwanted, isolated, and abandoned again. It was heartbreaking. Years of this would lead me to conclude that we would never get married, that I was never going to hear three little words from him. He rarely said it and when he did tell me he loved me it was usually fueled by alcohol.

Since I learned to be passive having conversations about my feelings didn't seem to be productive, walking on hot coals seemed easier than putting my feelings into words. It was easier for me to overlook the hurt and pain and continue to push it down into the already tangled weeds inside. By pushing everything down, I would walk on eggshells, trying not to rock the boat until things just worked. I avoided arguments and disagreements anything that would seem as if our relationship was rocky. The hopeless romantic inside held on to the hope that things would work themselves out, which if I did something well enough or did something that we would be okay and spend our lives together. I never communicated any of this I just kept holding out for change that would never occur because I never vocalized what I needed. By doing this I fulfilled my own fear that this would not work and I would be left alone again.

Chapter 7

"Until you make the unconscious conscious, it will direct your life and you will call it fate" - CG Jung

Prior to 2015, the only time I had remotely heard the word "therapy" was when it was rarely brought up by my family. I had always had an interest in psychology -- I love learning how the mind works and everything involved with personality, and abnormal psychology in relation to behavior. One summer possibly between middle school and high school, my dad was planning to take a couple of weeks to go help a friend in Northern Minnesota at his cabin. My dad was self-employed and installed windows, doors and did other home improvements.

I remember in our dining room my stepmother asked my "psychological" opinion about if a girl would need therapy because of her "unnatural attachment" to her dad. This was a loaded question; I knew damn well the question was about me. These couple of weeks without my dad would be the longest I had ever been away from him. I still remember my initial thought: "Bitch, *you* need therapy." I don't remember my response and I'm sure I said something snarky. I hated the question; I didn't know to answer it without pinning myself into a corner. I knew damn well I should be in therapy, but not because of my "unnatural" attachment to my dad -- because this woman seemed to believe there was something inappropriate between me and my dad.

After losing my mom to breast cancer, he was my primary caregiver. He filled both roles of mom and dad, so of course, I was attached to him. For a couple of years after losing my mom, it was just us. He had learned to curl my hair and not burn me and he would be my coach while playing t-ball. I had put the love I had for two parents into one. My stepmother seemed to feel because of this "unnatural" attachment; I needed to be in therapy as if something was wrong with me. He was my primary caregiver after my mom died; of course, I would be attached to him. What I had experienced when I was younger was traumatic and I clung to the only parent I knew left.

Once they got married, I spent less quality time with my dad. Even when I was in college he only came to visit me alone once and we went to get coffee. When we sat down the first thing out of his mouth was how sad my stepmother was that I didn't include her. Apparently spending one on one time together was not as high on his list of priorities. I would ask to spend some time together alone or just a phone conversation and he would always tell me how left out my stepmother would feel and how I needed to include her in everything. At one point it had gotten to where I would rarely talk to my dad on the phone, it was constantly my stepmother calling and relaying messages for him.

My therapist tried to help me re-establish a relationship with my dad, but it was met with some resistance from my both parents that I eventually gave up and put some distance between us.

I always knew I needed to be in therapy, probably since 7th or 8th grade. Maybe even younger, but let's go with that for now. By this time I had become an avid journaler. I wrote about everything and anything. It was my outlet for all the frustrations and hurt I had gone through. I have gone back several times and re-read old diaries and journals I kept throughout my adolescence and into college. I knew even then the anxiety, negative and irrational thoughts I was having weren't "normal." There are entries discussing therapy, depression and the high conflict relationship I had with my stepmother. I could never explain how or why I felt any of these things, I just knew that what I felt wasn't "normal." I was trying to figure out my place in a blended family while going through the awkward phase in middle school. It was a lonely place trying to navigate such a time in my life without knowing who to talk to or trusting that anyone would understand.

I remember when my friends would invite me somewhere -- a movie, the mall or even just over to their house during the summer. I had a habit of always being ready earlier than necessary. I remember one time specifically, I was ready and standing in my garage looking out to the driveway, getting anxious because I thought for sure my friends were playing a trick and only invited me out of pity, only to stand me up. I thought all of this because their mom was five minutes late picking me up. I remember calling their house and no one answered, which only confirmed my irrational thought that I must have been stood up. Just as I was about to turn my head and sulk back into the house, their mom's big brown van would pull up and my friends would be waiting. By this time I told myself that I am ridiculous and my thoughts are absolutely absurd. To this day, I still think that when I am invited somewhere, that it's out of pity, not because these people are my friends. It's still a daily struggle.

In fourth grade, that's when the severe separation anxiety set in, prior to that, in third grade I acted out with behaviors in the classroom. I am still embarrassed to this day when I think about that behavior. I don't even want to discuss it; I just remember I couldn't control my actions. Each morning my dad would drop me off at school and I would begin to sob uncontrollably asking for him to stay or to bring me with him. It was uncontrollable, *I* was uncontrollable. I didn't want him to leave; I didn't know if he would come back or if he would be okay if he wasn't near me all the time. I had some of the most patient teachers in 3rd and 4th grade. Looking back I am so embarrassed.

I couldn't even get out of my dad's truck to go to a friend's birthday party because I didn't want to be separated from him. There were so many events that I missed out on because I did not know how to regulate my emotions, It wasn't until my dad told me that "unless you stop acting like this you will have to be sent to a different school where they can handle these behaviors" that I tried to keep my emotions in check. That is not what I needed; no one ever wants to hear. I needed someone to care, someone to comfort me when I needed it. Thank you, Ms. McNamara, Mrs. Jeffrey, and Mrs. Deutsch, the three of you were some of the best teachers I have ever had. Thank you.

After that, I went to a "class" at our local hospital. It was called Rainbows, the class was for children who lost a parent or whose parents were going to divorce. Looking back it seemed more like a support group. Thankfully there was another girl, Alyssa from my school who had lost her father to cancer the summer after my mom. She and I had a special bond, we still do. We formed our own "club", obviously membership was involuntary and no one wanted to be a member, but it was our own and we were there for each other. She was one of the first people I ran to when I found out my dad was diagnosed with ALS and like a day had never gone by, she was there again.

She was such a comfort in grade school, my security blanket in a place that seemed unsafe to me. I went to a Catholic school and we would attend church every Wednesday. After I lost my mom, going to church and hearing some of the songs that were played at her funeral would send me back down spiraling. Thankfully Alyssa was there. She and I would be there to comfort each other. Sometimes we would use our circumstances just to go down to the bathroom and talk. The talks I don't remember, but the time together I will never forget.

During the third and fourth grade, she was my confidant, my rock and my support, as long as she was there; I knew I would be okay. We would sit near each other during church and cry if a certain song would come on or would walk to the bathroom when our classes were discussing something related to death or dying. To this day she means more to me than words would ever be able to explain. She knows what it is like, knows the struggle, the pain, the hurt and all the scars that we bare. As we grew older we were not in the same social circles and the only time we spent some time together was during our "religion" group in high school which was held in her home.

As most friendships do from childhood and high school we lost touch aside from Facebook during college and after. She never knew but I looked in from time to time on her Facebook. It was a comfort to me that she was there and that even if we never said it, that we were both still there because of each other.

During college my grades were not the best, in fact, they were downright embarrassing for me. I was a National Honor Society Member in high school and my grades in college; well let's just say that I was excited for being average. In the fall of my sophomore year, I began working with school aged children with special needs, specifically autism. I always joked that I had what I dubbed "music ADD" that I would listen to a part of a song and then skip around until I found another song and was constantly changing the radio, cd or iPod. One day just because it was a slow day at work and a coworker of mine had mentioned some ADD traits; I took an online ADD/ADHD screening test.

Now don't jump on me for this, I understand that using the internet to "self-diagnose" is not the smartest thing to do but it's what I had at the time. I remember calling my stepmother since I was still on her insurance and told her that I wanted to look into ADD/ADHD testing. That I was concerned because I had fit so many of the symptoms listen online. I remember bringing up the online screening, which probably wasn't the smartest idea but hell, what did I know?

I remember being met with resistance, little support and a comment was made that I shouldn't be looking for excuses as to why my grades were slipping. She kept telling me I just needed to study and concentrate more; the fact that there was even a possibility of me having ADD/ADHD was absurd. It was then brought to my attention since I can retain copious amount of random information then it must be because I am not paying attention, attending class or even studying. After that conversation, I knew my opinion wasn't important and advocating for myself was out of the question. I stopped my pursuit of therapy and testing for ADD.

From then on my opinions regarding my mental health or struggles were kept to either close friends or myself. I could not even talk to family about struggles or trials I was facing out of fear of additional judgment and criticism. My journal because my therapist, it was the place I could be myself, I would write before I ever talked to my family. I hid from them; I would try to convince them everything was fine, that I was just another 20 something going through 20 something struggles.

Pretending things were good then things must be good even if you are drowning on the inside. It was something that I eventually learned to despise. Pretending everything was sunshine on the outside became the norm for me even though I was screaming and dying inside.

Looking back I should have spoken up and been my own advocate. There are so many things that I would have done differently, so many hurts that could have been avoided. Maybe if I would have pushed for therapy on my own then I would have gotten the help I so desperately needed. Bringing up such a topic in my household seemed to either fall on deaf ears, looked at as an excuse or seen as me blaming others for my actions. I had a strained and rocky relationship with my stepmother, to begin with and my dad seemed to take more of a "behind the scenes" take to parenting. He would make comments here and there but never seemed assertive enough to have his opinion to be heard, unfortunately, this trait I inevitably picked up.

Why didn't anyone else reach out and notice I needed help? Did my teachers notice? I know they did when I was in third and fourth grade. I would act out behaviorally; I still don't know why and I am still ashamed and embarrassed to even talk about it. How could they not notice? I know they knew I know they saw a little girl that looked lost in the world and would cry at even the slightest discussion of death, certain songs at church or whenever her dad would drop her off at school. Did they ever say anything? Was my dad the resistant one? I may never know but I know now looking back I needed help then, I am just thankful that now I am getting the help I need.

Chapter 8

"How would you nurture her if you were the mother of little you?" - Kris Carr

Until now, I have never said this next part out loud. At my inner core, I am still the little girl standing next to her mom's grave, holding a teddy bear, sobbing and screaming at the top of her lungs, waiting for her dad to come and comfort her. I have been that little girl since I lost my mom, through grade school, middle school, high school, college and most of my adult life. This little girl needed someone to nurture here, to comfort her, to make her feel not so alone in the world. This root was the hardest to dig out and find. There have many times that I have tried to ignore this little girl or to appease her momentarily in hopes that I would able to silence her.

Now as an adult, I have to play the nurturing role and the adult role; I have to tell that little girl that it's going to be okay. Whether or not I believe myself I have to continue to care for this little girl, reminding her we are together and that I am never leaving. Some days I believe the nurturing words spoken to my inner child, other days it's a struggle. Some days I succumb to the little girl inside and I can't get out of bed. Slowly with baby steps, I have been able to heal from the inside out; I have slowly started to weed out these tangled and mangled roots.

It wasn't until I started getting involved in the KAD, Korean Adoptee community that I actually felt understood. I would read people's experiences and struggles and I would think to myself that there are people just like me out in the world, that I wasn't alone. My trials, feelings, and roots were not only specific to me but to other people as well. I cannot put into words what it felt like to find people who understood and were willing to be brave to talk about their problems, their baggage, and all the pain that came with it. When I started to interact with some of these people, mostly the women, there was this deep understanding even when we would just talk over text messages or phone calls.

One spring, there was a group of women that got together, I decided to join in. With my anxiety in the back of my head telling me that I wasn't going to fit it, I walked down the hotel hallway as nervous as a kindergartener going to school. Part of me wanted to turn and run away, to hit my panic button and find an excuse why I wasn't able to join them. Then I heard it, the sound of laughing and my anxiety dissipated and felt at ease. It was one of the weirdest experiences of my life. Instantly upon meeting these women there were feelings of being completely understood without having to express it, it was incredible. I had found people who just understood.

It wasn't until recently how much my self-sabotaging behavior really hurt those closest to me, or where it even came from. Finally, after years of not being able to pinpoint where all the anxiety and sporadic irrational and impulsive actions stemmed from, I finally had some answers. When I started therapy I had chosen a woman who typically worked with people in high conflict relationships. After starting therapy with her, I started to relearn myself. She would assign me homework and push me to dig deeper. It was her suggestion that I speak with my doctor about medication, something my family seems to frown upon. Once all the medication was at the therapeutic levels, I felt like a completely different person. I had more control over my impulses and overall felt like a fog had been lifted. How I managed to keep myself together through middle school, high school, and college I'll never know. This had been missing most of my life.

After a while my therapist and I dug into deeper issues, we discussed things happening in my life and skills that I needed to learn. She helped me decrease the amount of conflict that had run my life. I learned that it was okay to be selfish from time to time to work on myself, to take some time away and focus on self-care. That obviously did not sit well with my family. I recall when I was on the phone with my parents; I was so excited that I had finally found a medication that worked and a therapist who was helping me. It was mentioned how they didn't understand why I was on medication or if there would be a way for me to wean off if it, they didn't agree with my therapist and that I should not take her advice. Without starting a fight I simply said that she is a professional and I am going to do as she suggests with regard to the medication, I simply stated that I have not felt better and will continue to take it. This time they wouldn't sour my opinion about therapy or medication. I finally was able to advocate for myself, to stand up for the little girl sobbing inside.

While I was in 4th grade, maybe 5th, I was outside helping my dad do some yard work. He stopped and asked me what I thought about my then future stepmother, and he asked how I would feel if he were to ask her to marry him. I wanted my dad to be happy, (what kid wouldn't?), but it did not sit well in my gut. *She* did not sit well in my gut. There was something even then that alerted my "warning" button. People will say that I felt this way because I saw her as "replacing" my mom. Well, I'm here to tell you that I loved the first girlfriend my dad had after my mom died. I wanted them to get married. She did not force me to have a relationship with her and slowly integrated herself into our lives. She understood what she was getting herself into and she treated me very kindly. However, their relationship ended since she wanted things to get more serious and my dad was not ready.

My stepmother is a different story. After they decided they were going to get married or shortly after, it felt like she demanded that we (me) see "us" as a family, and at one point wanted me to call her "mom" to make us a "real" family. It was unnatural to me, as I had never been pressured to call someone else "mom." I remember the few times I did call her mom, it didn't feel right, I didn't see her as that role and my mom would forever be my mom. There would be no one would be able to replace her, I didn't want to replace her, I wanted an addition, not a substitution.

My feelings are still sensitive and I still have my moments where I get caught up in my anxiety, but now I have more good days than bad. With the years of therapy and the assistance of medication, I have learned better ways to take care of myself, to protect the little sobbing girl inside. Learning to meet your own needs and heal yourself is a scary journey, there have been nights where I have cried myself to sleep, and others where I go for a run because I am so mad that it is the only thing I can do from exploding. The void that I felt was something I needed to mend, without the assistance of others, without the dependence of friends or significant others but alone.

Today it seems like it is an impossible task, that someday I will habitually revert to my broken unmended self, but I know better, as my friend says, self-love is a marathon, not a sprint. Part of me wants a quick fix, to put a band aid on it and continue on with life but that isn't what is healthy, what is healthy is for me to take the time to run the marathon and finish the race laid out before me. Just like the Bermuda grass, it is impractical to cover the flower bed with plastic and kill the flowers along with the

Bermuda grass but tedious to dig it out. I don't want to kill the good parts of me, just the weed that has been growing and infiltrating my life.

Sometimes I found it hard to believe people actually tried to break down my walls and fill my void. These unbelievable people were willing to sacrifice themselves in an attempt to fix me. It was never their responsibility to heal my open wounds, it was mine; something that took me years to figure out on my own. I wish I would have known then to even speak with a guidance counselor in middle school or high school. Maybe things would have been different, maybe not. I cannot dwell on the past; it is something I cannot change. Instead, I choose to see the old wounds and scars as an experience I had to shape me into who I am today and a reminder not to repeat the past.

Thankfully after the amount of time I had put into therapy, Auntie's comment about the long car trip went unnoticed by me. At that moment it did not matter whether or not I had her approval, I was finally able to block out the excess noise. I wasn't there for her or her opinion, I didn't even ask for her opinion, I wanted my son and I wanted to spend a little extra time with my dad. I privately laughed at her comment at the ridiculousness of it all, if someone would have driven with me that would have been an issue. I knew that either way there had to be something to complain about, some criticism had to occur otherwise hell probably would have frozen over. It was half of a drive I had done numerous times on my own and this is the only time she had ever been concerned about me driving. The passive aggressive comments were about to begin and I had prepared myself. I had a plan, to spend time with my dad and my son and interact as little as possible with my aunts.

After getting through this weekend without much conflict I had never been prouder of myself. As I pulled out of the parking lot with my son in the backseat, I smiled from ear to ear. It was the first time in my life that I had been able to get through a weekend without my raging mad, wanting to scream and end up in another argument with my family.

It was only within the last year in part to my therapist to really shine the light on a lot of these weeds and help me pull them out. She would help me critically think about different scenarios, potential conversations and provide feedback on appropriate ways to handle conflict while still being able to have appropriate boundaries with my parents. Setting appropriate boundaries was probably the hardest; she would always tell me that fences make good neighbors.

Prior to this, I had never really set any boundaries with my family; mostly I just remained passive and would find new hiding spots for my journal. When I first started to set appropriate boundaries, I got a lot of pushback from my parents. They were confused and didn't understand why I didn't want to be enmeshed or codependent on them. Using the new skills I was working on helped to try and keep the conflict to a minimum even after the boundaries were established.

It was around this time OU (other uncle) started with his voicemails. When his number showed up on my cell phone, I didn't want to speak to him; I hadn't spoken to him in quite some time. The call when to voicemail and I was nervous to hear what he had to say. Basically, his voicemail stated that I must be on drugs because I'm so fucked up. He was displeased that I was not calling my dad every single day after he received his diagnosis and only someone who is on drugs, selfish and fucked up would do that. He then continued saying that my parents gave me a good life, that I should not punish my dad because I continue to have issues with my stepmother. He yelled that I should be repaying them because of the good life they gave me that they were owed that.

I never want to be the type of parent that expects something from their child in return for providing them a "good life"; those words have been uttered before by my aunts and uncles over the years while I was in high school, college and even recently. That isn't unconditional love…that is CONDITIONAL love, love based on what you do, that love is earned by works. Caring for my children is my responsibility, they don't need to do anything to earn my love and I refuse to raise my children believing they owe me something. Raising children is a parent's responsibility, we are their primary caregiver, and an example to show them what unconditional love is.

Since I have started this journey in therapy, I keep following each behavior, each little root only to find more and more roots to dig out. I'm not sure how I started looking into abandonment issues. Maybe it was because I was concerned about my daughter. At this point, I should probably discuss my little family's structure. I moved to South Carolina in 2010 halfway through my pregnancy with my boyfriend at the time. He was offered a job there and I took the chance to run and get out of the Midwest. Two years after living in South Carolina and after our son was born we talked about another child. However, he had gotten a vasectomy after our son was born so "naturally" conceiving was not a possibility. We also weren't married, weren't engaged, we were just living together raising our child together, "playing house". We decided that we would start fostering since private adoption is very expensive. In October 2014, we were placed with our first placement. She has stolen our hearts and we are blessed to be her forever home. My daughter has seen some things that no child should ever see and experience things that I will never be able to erase from her mind. Since my career background is in psychology and working with children I wanted to get her any and all the help that she needed.

By the time she had been in our home for two months, I wanted to get a therapist involved. At the time I was still resistant to the thought of therapy but I knew it was something she needed. I could continue wearing a fake smile, pretend everything was okay and make sure she didn't end up like me. I didn't want her to have to learn how to pretend to be happy. I wanted to make sure that she got the help she needed when it was needed. I refused to let her turn into a 30 something that finally figured out where all the issues stemmed from like me.

It started out small, I started researching what signs to look for, what behaviors to expect and the type of help she would most likely need. There are so many parallels I saw of my younger self in her and yet I continued to be naive to the fact that I too needed help then. Focusing on her and her needs was a lost easier than digging up all of my roots. I kick myself every time I think of how my life would be different if I had just reached out for help. I know that doesn't change where my life is now but I know that I never want to be that old person again. She is dead and someone better and healthier is going to continue on this journey.

Like most women, I could sit on Pintrest for hours. I was on Pintrest and I started searching for behaviors associated with abandonment. Here is where things really start to hit me hard. I start reading the different pins and all of a sudden it feels like I have been hit in the gut. I saw one and the first thing I thought to myself was, "Holy shit, that's me". Of course, once you start down that rabbit hole on Pintrest you just get stuck staring at your phone only to realize that your arms hurt and then you finally stop. From there and from my KAD groups, I came across a podcast featuring Susan Anderson. The podcast hit home with me so hard. This woman, whom I had never met, never heard of just described what I felt inside and gave reasons as to why it was happening. I couldn't get enough, down another rabbit hole I went. I ordered her book, *The Journey from Abandonment to Healing: Revised and Updated: Surviving Through and Recovering from the Five Stages That Accompany the Loss of Love*. I started reading it as soon as I could get my hands on it. In her book, she cites a workbook that she has as well. Naturally, I had to order that as well. I started working on the day I got it. Within 7 days I had gone through 7 chapters of the workbook. I deeper I got into the workbook the more I started to uncover about myself, some things I knew, and other things were new.

It's taken me a long time to be able to admit this about myself, but in terms of reassurance, I'm pretty needy. Some days my anxiety gets the best of me and I need an extra few words to know that I am cared about with those I am closest too. Other days I am okay and I can "roll with the punches". This self-realization didn't happen until just recently. Over the years with each heartbreak and rejection, my self-esteem just continued to plummet until there wasn't anything left except a smiling face with a scared little girl inside. Until the abandonment workbook, I didn't realize how desperate I was for someone to nurture me. Even when I was little while my mom was sick in the hospital I just wanted someone to comfort me. I think that is what I was trying to find. The thing is that she was right here in the mirror looking back at me every day.

I love my little family. I never expected to break apart something I had dreamed about my whole life. There were unresolved issues, unresolved pain and since I didn't like conflict, like any good abandoholic, I found something else, someone else willing to give me the attention I craved, where there wasn't conflict or unresolved pain. It was easy and convenient, there weren't unresolved issues or difficulty communicating but it broke my little family in too many pieces to pick up. I didn't care at the time because there was someone who gave me the attention and reassurance my decade long relationship was lacking. He didn't care that I was broken or that I had my cart of luggage, he had his own too but that didn't matter. He could talk about his feelings and be open about them. I wasn't told that I was wrong or I misunderstood something.

It was after I broke my little family I sought out therapy. It had gotten to the point in my little family that we were arguing constantly, fighting seemed to be the only way we could communicate. At rock bottom, I finally decided to find a therapist. At first, I wasn't sure what to look for or even the type of therapist I wanted. There were concerns from my parents about the type of relationship I was in, they thought I was being emotionally abused and controlled, I was not. Nothing like that had ever happened in my relationship. There were some things that I did want in a therapist, I preferred a female. As I searched, I found a woman whose focus in therapy with in high conflict relationships and at the time that seemed to be the majority of my relationships. When I scheduled the appointment I was nervous excited and somewhat relieved.

Going into the session I broke down I couldn't stop the tears from flowing. Everything about my relationship and cheating just poured out in tears sobs. The entire time I felt loss and at the same time as if a weight had been lifted off of my shoulders. Everything that had happened within the last several months spilled out, all the pain, hurt, regret, embarrassment, and shame. From then on I saw her weekly we worked on mindfulness, so I could make it through the day without crying. She pushed me, gave me homework and continued to encourage me; she is exactly what I needed. I was validated, not told that I was crazy or to toughen up my skin, we dug into so many issues and reasons why things had happened the way they did.

Chapter 9

"A true friend is someone who sees the pain in your eyes while everyone else believes the smile on your face"
- Unknown

The family is the one place that we are supposed to feel secure, our refuge, and a place where we feel safe. For me this was not the case, my family increased my anxiety, it would stress me out and after a couple of days, and it would affect my mental house. My refuge and my place to feel secure were typically found in my friends or in my journal. My friends are my family; the friends I made after I joined my sorority are my sisters. The friendships that I have had over the years were the one place that I felt I was understood and had the ability to be myself.

The summer before 7th grade was a summer that I would make one of the best friends I have had in my life. Her name is Brianne, we had known each other since we were just over a year, and we met in the park. Her father had been our family's vet since I can remember. Growing up when my dad would take our dogs to the vet I would tag along and play with Brianne and sometimes her sisters. As the years went on we attended preschool, grade school middle school and eventually high school together. This summer would be the one where we would become the closest when we would be considered Siamese twins conjoined at the phone.

That particular summer day, I would later find out that Brianne was just calling people to see if they wanted to hang out. Thankfully I was one of the people we called. From that summer until high school we were inseparable. There would be nights when we would spend most of the night on the phone, if we weren't able to do that, we would be writing pages of notes. Our notes would get so excessive; we finally decided on little notebooks that we would pass in between classes. Those notebooks were filled with our inside jokes and all of our thoughts. We had found a mutual love for most boy bands, TRL and writing stories. She was the first friend where I could truly be myself with and was able to share all of the pain, hurt and challenges I was facing at home.

Our friendship is something that I still cherish. Even though we are not as close as we used to be, I know that when we do have conversations, it is as a day never goes by. We will continue to send each other the latest updates on the Backstreet Boys, and every once in a while we will send each other something that only we would understand. The end of middle school was so much easier because I had her to confide in.

It was until college that I found that type of friendship again. Despite my intimidating demeanor while boasting about making a girl cry with just a look, I had found three other women who were similar to me. The three of us struggled to maintain friendships with other women and we were more tomboy than a girly girl. When we joined the sorority we were in the same pledge class, and after a sleepover involving tribal headdresses, we had found out moment to bond. As the years went by we were there for each other through cancer scares, broken wrists, graduating from college, graduate school, moving, babies and weddings.

These women are my sisters even though we are spread out in three different states, we always seem to be group text messaging, talking via Skype and on the rare occasion taking a girls' trip. Without their friendship, the college would have been a lonely experience.

As I've mentioned before once the move to South Carolina was completed making new friends was hard. Thankfully we had met another couple with a little girl that attended the same daycare as our son. She is also Korean and ironically enough her birthday and her daughter's birthday is around the same time as my son's. Had it not been for that daycare we never would have connected. Our friendships were the same as the ones we had in college or for me, even middle school or high school. These people didn't know our past and we had to get to know people all over again. At first, it was difficult, I remember us talking about how much I missed our friends, the ones that had known us for years and where we were comfortable. This new group was different, it wasn't like the friends we had in college and on some level, we had forgotten that we weren't in college anymore.

It wasn't until one of those friends went through a tragedy that I finally felt we had made a connection. We had spent several girls nights together, Super Bowls, Fourth of Julys, hockey games and nights out at the bar but this girl's night was different. My friend had recently lost her daughter to anencephaly and this girl's night we were finally able to talk about it. If you don't know what anencephaly is, look it up but this little girl touched so many lives, she is the reason why my friendship with her mom is as strong as it is now. I can't wait until I can thank her and hug her.

Losses were something that I could relate to and sympathize with. Previously making a connection with them seemed to be a struggle for me, their family is very close, the kind of close that I wished for my family. They were happy spending the majority of their time together and that seemed odd to me, trying to understand that was fascinating and intimidating all at the same time. When we would spend time with them and their family, I always felt a little self-conscious, as if they were able to see that I had been previously hurt and that somehow I was still damaged goods.

Looking back I know that was my insecurity, my anxiety talking. These people were nothing but welcoming and supportive and now it was time for me. Rachael and I sat there talking after everyone else had left girls' night. Through the tears, jokes, and wine we just sat there talking about her recent loss, I listened as she tried to make sense of everything and figure out her new found identity of a mother of a beautiful little girl and the mother of a daughter she lost. We talked till maybe three or four in the morning. Most of the time it was her talking and me just sitting there listening to her pain, being the friend that I knew I would have needed had that been me.

Finally have close to eight years in South Carolina, I have finally figured out where I belong. I have found a group of friends and the previous feeling of loneliness is a fading memory. Back in 2015, after finding a church where I had finally felt spiritually fed, I joined a small group. While I browsed through the different choices for women's groups, there was only one that fit my schedule the only catch was that it was at 6:30 in the morning. Anyone who knows me knows that I am the furthest thing from a morning person. Almost every morning I hit snooze on my alarm at least two or three times after staying up too late the night before somehow I manage to peel myself from my bed. The thought of having to get up and be awake at 6:30 was going to be a challenge in itself but I knew this was something I needed to do and take a step outside my comfort zone.

The first morning I went I was nervous. I drove up to the house and ironically enough it was in a neighborhood that we had walked through when we first moved to the South. We were walking that night pretending that we were buying one of those houses and commenting on the types of cabinets and drawer handles. As I put my place into the park I was not sure what to expect, I didn't know how old these women were and a small part of me was hitting my panic button to abort and crawl back into bed. I stepped through the doorway and walked into the kitchen greeted by some very awake and bubbly women. They were smiling and around my age, thankfully, however, I immediately became self-conscious since I was in sweatpants with my hair in a messy bun looking at two women who were nicely dressed in business attire with their hair done. My anxiety had taken over and I wondered if I would ever be able to relate to these women.

As we started that morning I began to feel at ease, we were going through our testimonies and I was to introduce myself. Out of nowhere, I poured out my heart, I opened up the fresh wounds from my mistake that broke my family part and immediately jumped into the tough conversation. These women knew nothing about me except what I had shared, I didn't want to start out masquerading around as I had previously, I wanted the real me to show. After I had finished my introduction I wasn't sure what to expect but I was met with such kindness and encouragement. Those ladies quickly became family, from the hundreds of text messages we would go through each day, to the nights out at dinner laughing until our bellies hurt, these are some pretty amazing ladies.

Since I joined that group we have stopped meeting in the morning and our group leader decided that her season as our group leader had come to an end. Thankfully I am still in touch with two of these women, one whom I speak to almost daily. These two women have seen me at my lowest, and have walked through the darkest valley with me during the last three years of my journey. They have seen the tears fall and heard the pain of my journey and yet they are still there armed with encouragement and love. During one the darkest parts of my life, when I lost my dad, they were there without sugar coating, without the clichés, they were my biggest support during that time. I have the best cheerleaders I ever could have imagined, even when it comes to hearing the tough things, their words of truth always from a place of love, without the judgment and criticism. They mean more to me then they will ever know I am truly thankful they are in my life and I am a better person because of them.

Chapter 10

"We must take adventures in order to know where we truly belong" – Unknown

The spring of 2018, I crossed two items off of my bucket list by taking my first international trip alone to South Korea. Since I was a baby when I came over to the states I have no memories of Korean or living in an orphanage. The only picture my mom and dad have of me in Korea was one the adoption agency sent them.

This trip was always something in the back of my mind that I wanted to take. Once my dad had mentioned that he wanted to go with him, I felt this was the time to take the trip. After several months after my dad's passing, I was mentally ready to go back. It seems morbid but I booked the ticket a month before my dad would pass, I didn't know it at the time but I had purchased travel insurance in case he would have made it to the spring.

Back in 2016, I had started searching for my birth mother; I had a name, birthday and location of where she was born with some details about her childhood. Hoping this was enough information I started my search through a couple different organizations in Korea. There were some horror stories and amazing reunification stories I had heard from other

KADs. They would remind me not to hope in a reunification and to remain a realist.

Upon receiving my Korean adoption file, the birthday of my birth mother was different, the months weren't the same. Originally I thought it was because of a mistranslation but after looking through the documents, I assumed that it was deliberately changed. This was not an uncommon practice for adoption agencies to change our stories or our biological birth parents information. Being that I am a baby of the 1980s, there was less speculation that my information had been deliberately changed since this mostly happened with those born in the 70s or earlier?

Since I was going to visit Korea in 2018, it was recommended by one organization to wait until I arrived in Korea. There were several conversations I had with friends as well that said searching would be a lot easier once I was able to visit. In 2017, I had been accepted to participate in an adoptee trip to Korea but due to my dad's health, I had to decline the ten-day trip.

There were so many things to get ready for this trip, I didn't have a passport at the time and I definitely didn't know what to expect once I got to Korea. During my months of preparation, I spoke with other adoptees that I am friends with who have been to Korea. It seemed like I was asking them hundreds of questions a day often repeating myself.

My biggest fear was language, I know very few words in Korean and even that I probably mispronounce. They reassured me that as long as I'm not in the countryside most people can at the very least speak broken English. While I would be over there, two other KADs, one that I had been speaking to for a couple of years would be there and we would be able to meet up. This trip was something I felt needed to be done on my own, but I jumped at the chance to be with other KADs.

The day of my flight I was beyond nervous, the town I grew up in is predominately white and I had never really been somewhere where I looked like everyone else. My flight was from South Carolina to Atlanta and then from Atlanta to Incheon Airport. After hearing some of the horror stories of such long flights in the economy I decided to upgrade on the long flight to Korea, it was the best money ever spent.

Once I had gotten to Atlanta, I made it to my gate and the ratio of Asians to white people drastically changed. There was a significantly less amount of white faces and for a moment a felt a little uncomfortable. After waiting for a couple of minutes the gate attendant accounted the flight had been delayed, for six hours. I was stuck in a terminal for six hours with my own thoughts and anxieties running through my head.

As I found a seat in the gate waiting for the area I was beginning to hear Korean being spoken around me. In preparation for the trip, I was watching a lot of Korean dramas and listening to k-pop music, hearing the language starting to feel familiar. I was able to hear the difference if Chinese or Japanese was spoken instead of Korean.

While I was in college, I went to a meeting for the Asian Pacific club, or the Korean American club, something like that. The first meeting was a couple of people, I felt judged, I hadn't immigrated here and my parents hadn't immigrated here, I was an adoptee standing alone. I could feel their eyes looking at me as if I was not one of them, that I was different and definitely not Asian enough to be a part of the club. Needless to say, I never went back, I couldn't take another place where I felt less than, my family was enough.

During my wait for my flight in Atlanta to the board, I felt those same eyes looking at me, their judgment searing into my skin. As I looked around I noticed that no one was looking at me, I had completely made this up in my head, or at least I didn't catch anyone looking at me. The anxiety I had previously felt in college around the other Asians had returned and suddenly became self-conscious about everything from my hair to my carryon bags. I tried to silence the negative voices in my head, went to grab a beer and went back to watching Korean dramas until the flight was boarding.

Once the plane had landed in Incheon, it was almost midnight, the sky was dark and I wasn't able to see much except for the lights on the runway. After exiting the plane I took a deep breath and walked to the motherland, a place I was returning too after leaving it when I was a baby. I wasn't sure what emotions I would feel after exiting the plane there was a screen above the doors saying "Welcome to Korea". By this time I had a huge smile on my face as I was walked through the terminal searching for baggage claim. I turned my head around and gazed at the place and the runaway, I could feel my face getting hot and tears filling my eyes. In my head I began to yell at myself, I didn't want to be the girl that cried in the terminal, but it was too late, my eyes had filled with tears.

When I arrived at baggage claim, the feelings inside had gone from anxiety to joy. I was amazed at seeing everyone around me actually look like me. It's an incredible feeling, being in a place where you blend into the crowd instead of standing out. I felt at ease knowing I could just disappear into the crowd. People take that for granted, it was an amazing feeling knowing that I wasn't just a Korean face in a sea of white faces. My heart was at peace and I felt a sense of belonging and home, I finally knew that I had been missing this part of me all along. As I rode in my taxi toward Itaewon somehow there was something familiar about Korea, maybe it was smells or sounds. Being so young I know that being able to remember anything would be impossible but somewhere deep within me recognized Korea, as if I had been there my entire life.

During my trip, I explored Seoul, went shopping in Myeongdong, stayed in Itaewon, visited the

DMZ and when to Gyeongbok Palace while wearing a hanbok. My friend helped me figure out the subway so I wouldn't get lost. I managed to go the wrong way only once in my ten-day stay. Some days I would just walk around Itaewon where I was staying and just people watch.

The neighborhood was fascinating when I booked the Airbnb that I was staying at, I didn't realize that Itaewon has a bigger international population. Of course, there were Korean restaurants there but also Thai, Mexican and Middle Eastern food. This was probably the only place I visited that was more mixed with other nationalities and ethnicities than the rest of Korea.

Part of my trip was dedicated to my birth mother search; I had been in contact with a gentleman, John with an organization which helps adoptees with reunification, who had also been in contact with a former police officer known for helping adoptees. The anticipation to meet them took over most of the trip, the meetings continued to be pushed back until I had only a few days left in the country.

One day I went to the agency where I was adopted from and got to see my Korean file. A couple of years ago I had requested a copy of the entire file, most of it was there but I found a few things I had never seen before. As I glanced through the file I ran across progress reports from my mom. It appeared she had to fill out these forms a couple of times after I had been placed with them. Halfway across the world, I saw my mom's handwriting, it was incredibly comforting and breathtaking. On the progress report were questions about my sleep schedule, feeding schedule, social interaction, and overall adjustment. If I didn't know my mom loved me her answers would have proved it to me, as I read through her answers in all of the progress reports you would have not found a more proud mom. My case manager made me a copy of those progress reports and gave me the extra pictures they had received from my parents.

With two days left of my trip the day had finally come where I would meet up with the former police officer, my friend Layne, his cameraman and my contact through the agency, John. Layne reunited with his birth mother a couple of years ago, he is having a documentary made about him, his story and adoptees and their journey. I had agreed to be filmed and tell part of my story.

By this time, there were two addresses as a potential home for the woman suspected to be my birth mother. Both the former police officer and John were rather optimistic because the woman who matched the name and birthday on my file was the only one in the country. I was feeling everything at once as we started the taxi ride to the first address. I wasn't sure what to expect and Layne and I were discussing possible outcomes as I tried to keep my expectations low.

Single mothers, women who may have had children out of wedlock or put children up for adoption are still stigmatized in Korean culture.

Some of these women got married later in life and never told their husband that had given a child up for adoption. It was not uncommon for adoptees to find their birth mother only to be re-traumatized because she would not acknowledge them. This was something that I would have to prepare myself for as well as this woman not being the right woman. How do you not have hope that the first one was the right one? Inside I had a tiny voice hopeful that we had found her.

Since the stigma is still prevalent in Korean culture, the former police officer felt it was for the best if he were to approach the woman first while the rest of us stood back. He was unsure of the type of reaction he would get, there was everything from a slammed the door in the face to blatant lies being told to his face. As he walked up to the door I put my head down, the anticipation was overwhelming, I didn't know what to hope for, I didn't know what emotions to feel, I felt nothing and everything all at the same time. I could hear him speaking and responding to him was a female voice, I didn't know what they were saying but this made me all the more hopeful. After what seemed like an hour, he waved over John, pulled him aside and spoke some to him until we were finally waved over as well.

This moment I had been preparing for in therapy prior to leaving for the trip. I tried to keep my thoughts positive and realistic all at the same time. I knew that not all reunifications end like fairy tales if a reunification happens at all. My feelings were all over the place, I was excited, scared and fearful with millions of different questions swirling around in my head. My biggest fear and the thought I continued to push out of my head was being rejected yet again but by a parent this time, one that I didn't even know. The fear was overwhelming, but not knowing who this woman was even more unbearable. After a childhood of loss, I figured that if I was able to heal from those, if this one ended as a loss, I would be able to heal from that as well.

By the time I had managed to walk to where everyone was standing my heart was pounding so hard I could feel it in my ears. This was a moment I had only dreamed about and it was about to become a reality. I had intentionally looked at the ground out of fear since I did not know what I would expect once I lifted my eyes. I had come so far now was not a moment to lose strength. Slowly I lifted my eyes and saw the woman standing in front of me and immediately I knew. She was taller than me by a couple of inches, with an oval and narrow face, her body was slender build like mine but it was not my mother. The feeling was instant. The documents that I have stated that my mother is approx. 5ft, this woman stood taller than that.

In speaking with others KADs, some mentioned that they just knew it was their biological mother or father. That this overwhelming feeling came over them where they didn't question the biological connection. Immediately upon looking at this woman, I knew she was not my mother and my heart sank a little.

She was a very sweet woman, who was very eager to talk to us. It is also not unheard of that Koreans will not speak to strangers or close the door in people's faces so this was exceptional. She mentioned that she grew up in Busan and not from the area where my birth mother is from. She continued to say that an agency had already contacted her and she told her that she is not the woman I have been searching for. The name and birthday on my adoption record only match one woman in the country, this woman but it did not match up. She mentions that she has children but none that are my age, and then said she wishes that she was my mother and continued saying that she will pray for me and mother, that we will be able to reunite. She said that my mother would be proud that I grew up so well and pretty. As we left she gave me her number and told me to stop by next time I am in Seoul. This could not have gone any better unless she had been the one.

We said our goodbyes and she went back to her apartment. While talking with John and the former police officer, both were sure that this woman would be it. After reuniting many families the former police officer felt that this woman was truthful. With knowing that he mentioned that he is very interested to get to the bottom of who my birth mother is because there was so much detail left about her childhood. As John translated he stated that over the course of a couple of weeks, the former police officer is going to go to the province where my mother grew up and speak to some of the older men and women to see if they remember anything about my mother's story. Casually I mention that I have two different birthdays for my birth mother, as John translated we find out that they only had one birthday, I gave them the other date and I was told John would be in touch within the next couple of weeks.

Even with just a ten-day trip, flying back to the States was difficult. Once I reached the Incheon Airport after my last taxi ride in Seoul, I no longer only heard Korean being spoken, I also heard English. It sounded foreign to me, even though I had spoken it with my friends and when I would talk to my kids back home, it still sounded odd.

By the time I landed in Atlanta, I knew I was back to a place that would now seem foreign to me. As I looked around waiting to go through customs I no longer blended into the crowd, people seemed taller and once again I was a Korean face in a sea of white faces. The day after I got back from the trip I was going back to work, thankfully my sleep wasn't too off and I was able to get some rest.

After the trip, it was hard to adjust back to life in a society that I always stuck out in. There would be moments during the day when a wave of sadness just washed over me. I reached out to a couple of KADs and they confirmed that it was the post-Korea funk; most KADs would get that after going to Korea. Thankfully they mentioned the feelings of depression would pass and to eat a lot of Korean food and watch a lot of Korean dramas and that would help ease the pain. A few days after I had returned I was at work crying at my desk for no reason, just because I was said to be back home, even though now home was in two different places.

The trip was life-changing; I never knew there was a missing piece until I first stepped onto Korean soil. It was the strangest feeling having a place that I don't remember consider feeling like home. Even without being able to speak the language or understand every little cultural difference it was comforting to be there just like home. All of my life I never knew that returning back to Korea was something that I needed, something that would help heal the very primal wound of when I was first separated from my birth mother. Experiencing the little in Korea that I did help immensely with self-identity.

Weeks after the trip, I reached back out to John, asking if there had been any news on the search. He did not answer after a couple of weeks so I emailed him again. He responded saying that the former police officer is extremely busy and has not returned his emails. Reading that was very hard, I had gotten my hopes up that something would be found, that someone would be found.

Before I left, I left a sample of my DNA with the Korea police missing person department, in the hopes that if there is a match found, I will be notified. I have also done DNA testing in the States and have found several distant cousins. Honestly holding out to the hope that someone will be found sometimes drives me crazy. The sheer thought of finding such a biological connection sometimes makes my head spin.

Searching for a birth family is still very important to me, even if there remain unanswered questions. Until I am comfortable enough to be okay with unanswered questions, I have decided to stop searching and reaching out to John. At this point in my life pursuing this search will most likely do more harm than good. I am still healing from losing my dad and I am not sure I could handle another rejection or let down so soon after. If I am to be reunited, I know it will happen, and then I am ready again I will start the search again.

Chapter 11

"The poison leaves bit by bit, not all at once. Be patient. You are healing." - Unknown

Looking back on my past, my painful decisions, broken hearts and outrageous behaviors is painful. There are things I wish I could change, words that I wish would be forgotten and other decisions that I will forever regret. Dwelling on the pain of the past, the sting of regret and the bitterness of unkind words will only hinder any progress that I have made. Moving forward requires having to leave what has happened behind, brush yourself off when you have fallen and continue to move forward. I may never be able to forget what has happened what hurts that have happened to me, but I can forgive those who have hurt me and chose not to continue making them a part of my thoughts. To continue to let such hurtful things cloud your mind will only end up hurting the one person trying to heal, yourself.

It is a slow painful process. Days come and go where all you can think about is who previously hurt you, or words that you want to be able to take back when the weight of the anxiety clouds your judgment and it is hard to see through the fog. On those types of days, the journey to healing is a struggle; those are the days where I want to give up, giving in to the temptation to the dark swirling abyss.

It remains uncomfortable to admit at the heart of everything you are just a scared little girl wanting someone to love, nurture and comfort her. I don't like admitting it to myself, in fact, it's hard. Exposing your darkest secret to the world knowing with one word someone can make your world come crashing down again. It's painful to go back when those moments of rejection flood your memory and remembering how much you love yourself is the most difficult thing you can think of. I have to stop myself from recalling every insult, critical comment or breakup from infecting my daily thoughts. Some days are worse than others. Some days the past comes hitting me from behind and knocks the wind out of my chest. Other days I feel like I have climbed a mountain.

My little family is still broken and it was not until recently that I really found the root of all my unhappiness and self-destructive behavior. I've known it's been there for a long time, longer than I would like to admit, but it is there. The pain and the primal wound have been ignored long enough and the little girl inside needs me to be the nurturing unconditional loving parent that she needs to thrive.

The issues have been pushed down so far that bringing them up stirs a bit of uncomfortableness; they had become a part of me, just like the Bermuda grass had become part of the flower bed. Just like the Bermuda grass, the core issues need to be pulled out, every extra little root and rhizome. I have to dig deep and learn new things about myself and learn to love myself to heal from the inside out.

With the multitude of insecurities rooted in childhood that have shaped my self-esteem that it is time to dig them out, just like the Bermuda grass. I had to find each root and follow it to the source so it could be brought into the light and eradicated. The most challenging part was where to begin, which issue or root was I going to dig out first. In time I figured starting anywhere was better than not starting at all.

At first taking on such dark and deep seeded issues was intimidating and overwhelming. As I started to go through and identify everything that I had experienced and began connecting past experiences with current behavior the thought of finally healing from everything was quite daunting. During some of this time, I reached out to my mom's cousin, someone that knew her very well. From time to time I would ask questions about her or ask to hear another story about her. I loved reading the stories and hearing about her during high school.

One evening I was going through some of her things that my dad had brought down to me. There were old wedding photos of them, graduation pictures, and a scrapbook. While flipping through old report cards and other achievements, I found a copy of her commencement speech. Up until this moment I didn't know my mom liked to write, she was amazing. Her speech talked about courage and that courage does not require anything special or supernatural. She stated that within us lies incredible strength and courage.

That evening was difficult; I had been exceptionally hard on myself and had succumbed to the overwhelming anxiety. As she gave this speech to her graduating high school class I doubt she ever thought that it would continue to impact people's lives, specifically mine. Something happened that night, I had a fight through within me that I hadn't felt or at least don't remember ever feeling. It was a fight to survive, to thrive and to become better and to heal from old wounds.

Throughout this journey, I had to learn to love myself, to believe that I was worthy of love which continues to be a struggle. Those who self-sabotage do so because they do not feel as if they are worthy enough to be loved or cared for. The vulnerability of letting someone love us magnifies our insecurities so we sabotage our something great because we choose to believe we are less than.

As someone who used to boast of how comfortable I was with myself or how much I loved myself, I never fooled myself. During this journey, I've had to face the reality head-on. My life had been filled with rejection, criticism, loss, and lack of nurturing I believed that I wasn't worthy of something great. My distorted view of myself caused reckless and impulsive behavior. The more serious something was the most reckless my behavior would become and the less I was aware of it.

This healing takes a long time, it will probably take as long to heal as it did to create this. No matter how much I want it to happen overnight, I have to remember to trust the process and continue moving forward. I don't know the destination I am going and that's okay. Ahead of me, there is going to be more loss, rejection, and criticism and I'm prepared for that. When I look in the mirror I don't see the mask I used to time behind, I see a warrior. One that has conquered everything life has thrown at her.

This self-healing journey is a lot of work, some days I feel like I have moved leaps and bounds then others feel like I have taken a hundred steps back. It seems like there are days where I can feel invincible as if I have figured everything out. However, once the Bermuda grass was pulled out of the flower beds, the soil wasn't the same. It had been disturbed and would still look the same but its composition had changed.

Most days it's hard to remember that, I am not who I was and I have been changed. I don't really know what "normal" is. I don't know what it's not like to try and self-sabotage something good, hell I'm still catching myself doing it. I don't know what it feels like to be normal, I have never been normal per se. I am learning who I am without being knotted up and tangled in weeds.

My healing journey has been just that, a journey. It has not been easy and along the way, I have had many detours, forks in the road and dead ends. There are times that I want to give up, and then I look at both of my children and realize that I don't want them to have a broken mom or to end up with the hurts that I have endured, so I press on. My children deserve a mom who will show them to be strong and look forward instead of continuously looking back with the pains of regret. I have stumbled over my own feet, gotten lost along the way, tripped and fallen flat on my face but I continue on this lifelong journey. I would have not become who I am today without all of those detours, dead ends, and falls.